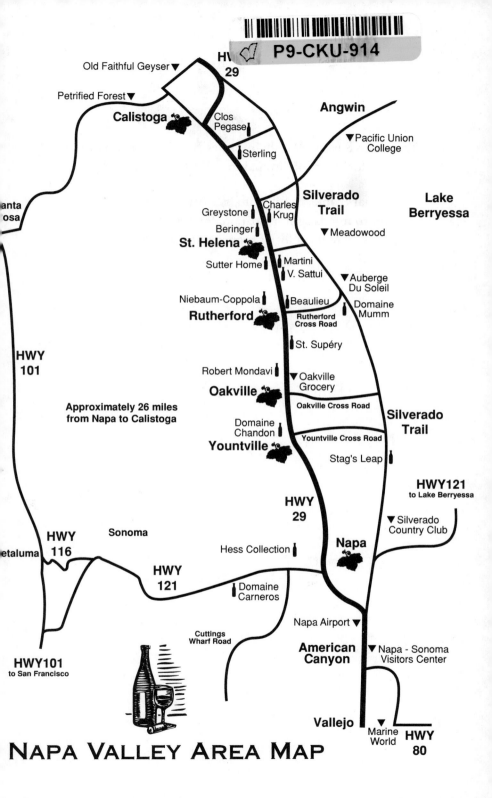

P9-CKU-914

HWY 29

Old Faithful Geyser ▼

Petrified Forest ▼

Calistoga

Clos Pegase

Sterling

Angwin

▼ Pacific Union College

Silverado Trail

Greystone

Charles Krug

Beringer

St. Helena

Sutter Home

Martini

V. Sattui

▼ Meadowood

▼ Auberge Du Soleil

Niebaum-Coppola

Beaulieu

Rutherford

Rutherford Cross Road

Domaine Mumm

St. Supéry

Lake Berryessa

anta osa

Robert Mondavi

▼ Oakville Grocery

Oakville

HWY 101

Approximately 26 miles from Napa to Calistoga

Oakville Cross Road

Domaine Chandon

Yountville Cross Road

Silverado Trail

Yountville

Stag's Leap

HWY121
to Lake Berryessa

HWY 29

Sonoma

HWY 116

etaluma

Hess Collection

HWY 121

Domaine Carneros

▼ Silverado Country Club

Napa

Napa Airport ▼

Cuttings Wharf Road

American Canyon

▼ Napa - Sonoma Visitors Center

HWY101
to San Francisco

Vallejo

▼ Marine World

HWY 80

NAPA VALLEY AREA MAP

Thanks to Shauna Marshall, James Brown, and David Howe
for their role in making this book a reality.

Special thanks to my wife, Kathryn, for her patience,
and to my daughter, Joanna, for her encouragement:
"Make a lot of money with it , Dad!"

NAPA VALLEY IN A NUTSHELL

An Insider's Guide to the 100 Best Napa Valley Experiences

Mick Winter

Westsong Publishing, Napa, CA

NAPA VALLEY IN A NUTSHELL

An Insider's Guide to the 100 Best Napa Valley Experiences

by Mick Winter

Published by:

Westsong Publishing
PO Box 2254
Napa CA 94558
www.westsong.com/pub

ISBN 0-9659000-0-2

Cover and book designed by:
Shauna Marshall

Printed in the United States of America

TABLE OF CONTENTS

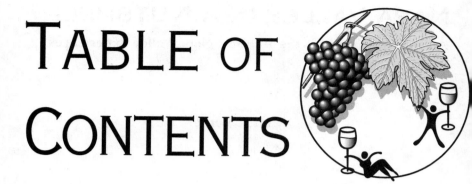

WELCOME TO THE NAPA VALLEY

TOUR SUGGESTIONS

THE "100 BEST"

SCENIC DRIVES

SPECIAL FEATURES

WELCOME TO THE NAPA VALLEY

We live here.

Over the years, watching visitors come and go, we've realized how helpful it would be if they knew what was the very best to see and do in the Napa Valley.

If you're here for only a day or two, as are 90% of the visitors to our valley, you don't have time to visit every one of the more than 200 wineries in Napa County, or to eat at every one of our fine restaurants. And then there's shopping, hiking, golf, ballooning, spas, music, gliding, entertainment and more.

To make your visit easier, we've listed what we feel are the very best, most unusual, most interesting, most enjoyable and most varied Napa Valley experiences. The rest is up to you.

We'd like to thank our volunteer panel of Napa Valley residents for their advice in determining our top 100 listings. Their collective wisdom was of great help. Of course, just because we limited our selection to 100 doesn't mean there isn't anything else worth seeing. Every one of the wineries in the Napa Valley makes outstanding wine. Believe us, we've tried almost all of them. For our 100 Best section, we've selected the wineries that are perennial visitor favorites, and included others that have some unique quality or offering we felt you would enjoy.

The same with restaurants. We may be a small rural area, but we're blessed with a large number of truly first-class restaurants. Here again we've listed some of the best known and added others known pretty much only to locals. But there are many, many others that deserve your patronage, many with worldwide reputations.

As we have no ads, you can be sure that all of our listings are based totally on what we believe is their value to you, the visitor to the Napa Valley. We hope we're able to help you enjoy your visit, whether it's for a day, a weekend, or longer.

We welcome any comments, suggestions and recommendations you have. If you found one of our listings unsatisfactory, we definitely want to know. And if you discovered a place or activity you feel should be included in our next edition, we want to know that, too. You can email us at nutshell@westsong.com or drop us a line at:

Nutshell
PO Box 2254
Napa CA 94558

Thanks for buying our book. We wish you great enjoyment as you visit our home — the beautiful Napa Valley.

Mick Winter & Friends

WHERE IS THE NAPA VALLEY?

It's in Northern California at the northeastern tip of San Francisco Bay (actually called San Pablo Bay up that far), about an hour's drive north of San Francisco. To the west is the Sonoma Valley, to the east is Lake Berryessa and Yolo and Solano Counties, and to the north Lake County. The Napa Valley is actually just one of many valleys in Napa County, but it's by far the largest and best known. The valley itself is about 30 miles long and ranges from one to five miles wide.

Napa County has a population of about 110,000 people, and five incorporated cities. North to South, they are: Calistoga,St. Helena, Yountville, Napa and, at the southern end, American Canyon. Angwin, Rutherford and Oakville are communities with post offices but aren't actual towns.

The county's primary industries are winegrape growing, wine production and tourism. Thanks to stringent and ongoing efforts by the vast majority of the voters, there is little development in the county itself; most commercial and residential development is in the cities. This preserves a huge amount of agricultural land, allowing Napa County to avoid the urban sprawl that has affected almost all other San Francisco Bay Area counties. The result is an attractive place for residents to live and tourists to visit.

TRANSPORTATION

You can reach the Napa Valley by air, land or water. However, because there is no scheduled service to the Napa County Airport (visitors arrive by private plane or charter), few come by water (the ferry takes you only as far as Vallejo, although small boats can go up the Napa River as far as the city of Napa), and over 90% of our visitors come by car or tour bus, we'll focus on arriving by land.

FROM SAN FRANCISCO

Drive north over the Golden Gate Bridge on Highway 101 almost to Novato, take the Napa (Highway 37) exit to Highway 121/12 and continue following the signs to Napa. The trip takes just under an hour in good traffic, considerably more at rush hour. But as a visitor you shouldn't be driving at rush hour anyhow. Enjoy the views, the cows, the vineyards, the oak trees. It's by far the most scenic way to drive to the Napa Valley.

Shortly before you reach the Napa Valley, you'll pass (on the right side of Highway 121– the Carneros Highway) Domaine Carneros winery. The chateau is inspired by the Chateau de la Marquetterie, the historic 18th century Champagne residence owned by the principal founder of Domaine Carneros, Champagne Tattinger of Reims, France.

A short time later you'll find yourself at Highway 29, the main highway running north-south in the valley. Turn left (north) toward Napa and Calistoga.

FROM OAKLAND AND SACRAMENTO

Take Interstate 80 north from Oakland or west from Sacramento. If you're staying right downtown in San Francisco, it's usually quicker this way — over the Bay Bridge — than going through town and over the Golden Gate Bridge. Going up the East Bay isn't pretty, but it's fast.

Turn off Highway 80 at the Napa exit and head toward the Napa Valley. At some point you'll pass the intersection of Highway 29 and Highway 12. At the southeast corner of this intersection, across from the Napa County Airport, is a large three story stone building nestled among oak trees that looks like it just has to be a winery. It isn't. It's an insurance company. Sorry — no visitors, no wine, and no picnicking.

HEY, DID YOU SEE THOSE FUNNY LOOKING COWS?

Just after you head up Highway 29 you may see some cows on your left. These black cows with white belts are called "Dutch belted" cows. They're raised for both beef and milk. (If you want to double back for a better look, take the Imola Avenue turnoff, go over the highway, then drive back south on the frontage road.)

On the other side of Highway 29 is the Napa County Airport. The largest facility there belongs to Japan Air Lines. They provide basic flight training for almost all their pilots here. More than 150 student pilots are undergoing training at any given time.

Continuing north, you'll come to a fork. You can either go right onto Soscol Avenue (forking off to the right just before the traffic light) and on into the town of Napa, or go left over the Southern Crossing (George F. Butler Bridge) and continue north on Highway 29 toward Calistoga. (From 29 there are a number of exits into Napa). It's your choice, although we suggest you follow the "Calistoga" sign and stay on 29. It's a much prettier drive. If you do, as you cross the bridge you'll look down on the meandering Napa River.

NAPA RIVER

The Napa River is one of four navigable rivers in California. It's a major source of freshwater to San Francisco Bay, and offers excellent fishing for striped bass and sturgeon. There's even peaceful canoeing right in the heart of Napa. It's also the home river for the "City of Napa", Napa's sternwheeler riverboat.

Currently a local organization, "Friends of the Napa River", has formed to preserve the river, which has a tendency to frequently flood downtown Napa. Of course building a city on a flood plain wasn't a great idea to begin with, but now that it's here, citizens are creating ways to save both the river and the city by turning out a river that's developed and flood-safe, yet still natural and free-flowing.

HISTORY

The original inhabitants of the valley were the Wappo. The name Wappo was given by the Spanish and probably derived from the Spanish word "guapo" meaning "handsome." The natives were here at least 4,000 years before the Spaniards arrived. In 1831 there were an estimated 10,000 to 12,000 Wappo living in the valley. Most later lost their lives to cholera and smallpox, as well as to attacks by white men. There are still surviving Wappo in Napa, Sonoma and Lake counties.

The first American settler in the Napa Valley was George Yount. He arrived in 1831, became friends with General Mariano Vallejo, and was given an 11,000 acre Mexican land grant. He built the first wooden structure in the county, a two-story Kentucky block house. He also planted the first grapevines in the Napa Valley. The vines were from Mexico; it was not until 1860 that the higher quality European winegrapes were introduced.

The wealth of post-Gold Rush San Francisco created a huge demand for wine, and by 1891 there were 619 vineyards throughout the valley. The wineries survived economic depression and the disease of phylloxera but were no match for Prohibition, the United States' "Great Experiment" of declaring alcoholic beverages not just immoral but illegal. Prohibition closed almost every Napa Valley winery. The few that survived provided medicinal wine or sacramental wine for churches. Vineyards were ripped out, to be replaced by prune and walnut orchards.

Prohibition ended in 1933, but it was not until 1966 that a new winery was finally built in the Napa Valley. It was Robert Mondavi Winery in Oakville. Since that time several hundred wineries have been built, as the Napa Valley was rediscovered as a premium wine region, recapturing its earlier pre-Prohibition fame. Today there are more than 200 wineries throughout the county.

VOLCANO? WHAT VOLCANO?

That extinct volcano you see at the north end of the valley — Mount St. Helena — is not extinct. But not to worry, it isn't a volcano either. Despite the beliefs of many locals, it's just a mountain. It is, however, one of the four dominant mountains of the San Francisco Bay Area. Mount St. Helena at the north; Mount Hamilton at the south — near San Jose; Mount Diablo at the east — near Concord; and Mount Tamalpais at the west in Marin County.

Even if Mount St. Helena was never a volcano, there is a great deal of geyser activity just below it in the hot springs town of Calistoga, and to the northwest in an area known as The Geysers, currently used as a source of thermal energy by Pacific Gas and Electric Company.

THE NAPA VALLEY TODAY

Today the Napa Valley is one of the most popular tourist attractions in California, and world renowned for its wines. The fame of its wineries is matched by the reputation of its restaurants. Combined with the beauty of the area, they provide a vacation holiday without equal anywhere in the country.

Although many locals like to say that the Napa Valley gets as many visitors as Disneyland, the reality is that Disneyland has about 14 million visitors a year and the Napa Valley a little over five million. Five million is enough — particularly because most of them come either during the summer or during "crush", the harvest in September and October. Come visit us during late fall, over the winter, or in the spring and you'll find far fewer people and have much more time to chat with winery staff. The valley is beautiful all year long, just different from season to season. The wine is always delicious.

THE WINES OF THE NAPA VALLEY

The Napa Valley's climate and soil have made it one of the world's great wine growing regions. It has long been famous for its ability to grow Bordeaux grapes such as Cabernet Sauvignon and Sauvignon Blanc. Later it was discovered that the southern part of the valley, particularly the Carneros region next to the San Francisco Bay, was ideal for growing the grapes of Burgundy, including Chardonnay and Pinot Noir.

Other popular wines include Merlot, Zinfandel, Riesling, Petite Sirah, Gamay Beaujolais and Chenin Blanc, and some wineries are producing Semillon, Gamay, Cabernet Franc and Muscat. Recently there has been a return to the old Italian grapes that were once grown in the valley and wineries are beginning to produce such wines as Pinot Grigio, Sangiovese and Dolcetto.

There are also a small number of wineries that produce sparkling wine. Technically a sparkling wine has to be produced in the Champagne district of France to be called "Champagne", but because the United States never signed the international accord agreeing to that, some Napa Valley wineries call their product "champagne". Others honor the agreement and refer to their products as "sparkling wine."

ROMANTIC TIPS

More than half of the people who visit the Napa Valley arrive in pairs. With good reason: the Napa Valley is a romantic place. The views are gorgeous, the wine is both soothing and stimulating, the dining can be intimate and is always superb, the lodging is luxurious, and the mud baths, whirlpools and massages bring your body to full, tingling alert.

Is there something special a couple should do in the Napa Valley? Actually a visit to the valley is almost foolproof for romance. But we can provide a few pointers.

- Arrive in the valley in time for lunch, buy some goodies at one of the excellent delicatessens in this book, and picnic somewhere lovely and private. Or, as an alternative, you could have lunch on the Wine Train.

- Visit one or two wineries in the afternoon, but no more.

- Spend a couple of hours at a Calistoga spa, preferably one that allows the two of you to take a mud bath, mineral bath and massage in the same private room.

- Have a light dinner with just enough wine to feel very relaxed.

- Stroll the sidewalks of Calistoga for a little fresh air and to work off the dessert you might have had after dinner.

- Return to your room at one of the many hotels, B&Bs and resorts that offer rooms with their own whirlpool baths.

- Pop open a bottle of champagne, pour two glasses and, while soaking in your bubbling bath, toast each other for your good sense in coming to the Napa Valley.

The rest is up to you.

PHOTO OPS

You can take beautiful photographs anywhere in the Napa Valley. The following are some of the most popular locations for photos.

- Beringer Vineyards (St. Helena)

- Culinary Institute of America - Greystone (St. Helena)

- Old Faithful Geyser (Calistoga)

- Robert Mondavi Winery (Oakville)

- Sterling Vineyards (Calistoga)

- "The wine is bottled poetry" sign (Between Yountville and Oakville on West side of Highway 29)

DRIVE-IT-YOURSELF TOURS

THE "I'M JUST PASSING THROUGH"

If you're just passing through the Napa Valley, heading north or south to get somewhere else, try this tour. It's set up for those driving south to north through the valley. Simply reverse it if you're heading the other direction.

However you approach the valley from the south, head north on Highway 29. Pass through Napa and continue north till you come to Yountville. Take the Washington Street turnoff, turn right at the stop sign, then immediately left at the next stop sign. Continue into town, staying on the left at the fork. You'll find yourself at Vintage 1870, 40 shops in a three-story brick building on the west side of Washington Street. Stop, park, shop and/or have lunch. (If there's no time, just keep on driving through Yountville and pick up the directions in the next paragraph). You can eat lunch at Kinyon at Vintage 1870; just south across the street at Piatti's or The Diner; just north of Vintage at Compadre's; or at the north end of town at either the Napa Valley Grille or Frankie, Johnnie and Luigi's Too.

After lunch, continue north on Washington Street. Turn left at Madison Street (there's a stop sign there) to Highway 29. Very carefully turn right on the highway and head north. Approximately two miles ahead, just past Oakville, you'll see Robert Mondavi Winery on the left. Go into the left turn lane, then head into the winery. Park in the visitor's area. If there's time, take a tour. Otherwise just taste a few wines, take a few photographs, and head north again.

A few miles further north and you'll be in Rutherford. Just past the Rutherford Cross Road and the Rutherford Grill restaurant, pull into the Beaulieu Vineyard parking lot. Taste a few complimentary wines from this nearly 100-year-old winery. If you have the time, and the next tour is soon, take it. It's an excellent tour of wonderfully wine-smelling cellars and aging areas.

After BV, head north and drive through the town of St. Helena. Admire the quaintness of the town and overlook the fact that having a main highway through your quaint town is a traffic nightmare. Continue through town, take a picture out the window as you pass Beringer Vineyards and the Culinary Institute of America–Greystone on your left just north of town.

Continue a few more miles till you reach Calistoga. Turn right on Lincoln Avenue and drive into the heart of Calistoga's main shopping area. Here you can window shop, have an ice cream cone or cold beer (it's not all wine here), or if you've suddenly decided you're not in so much of a hurry, visit a spa and have a mud bath and massage. Your "I'm Just Passing Through" tour is over and you're on your own.

THE "FIVE HOUR"

Head up Highway 29 until you're just north of Oakville. Visit Robert Mondavi Winery on the left (west) side of the highway. Take a tour, taste some wine. It's the first of the new Napa Valley wineries; that is, it was built in 1966, the first winery built in the valley after Prohibition. Since Mondavi, several hundred others have appeared.

Leave Mondavi, turn left on Highway 29 and continue north. Just past the Rutherford Cross Road, turn right into Beaulieu Vineyard. This is the true monarch of the valley, built in 1900 and famous for its wines, particularly its Cabernet Sauvignon. Taste a variety of their complimentary wines, then tour the winery and experience the nearly 100-year-old buildings. This place looks and smells like a winery. It's wonderful.

After BV, keep your car in the parking lot and walk into the Rutherford Grill for lunch. Good food, extremely varied menu, and very casual and comfortable. Good place for kids too.

After lunch, continue north on Highway 29 and go into St. Helena. Wander around, enjoy the window shopping, maybe even buy something. There are top-notch stores for all tastes.

Leave St. Helena and head back south. If you still have time, you can visit another winery, shop at Vintage 1870 in Yountville, or visit Moet et Chandon's Domaine Chandon sparkling wine facilities (also in Yountville but on the west side of the highway).

We mentioned the view? It's everywhere. Highway 29 is an incredibly scenic highway and you'll see wineries and vineyards galore on the entire stretch.

Enjoy.

THE "FIRST TIMER - ALL DAY"

Most first-time visitors tend to start at the bottom of valley and work their way north, generally visiting wineries on the right-hand (east) side of the road. We suggest you skip the crowds and drive directly (but enjoy the view) to Rutherford. Visit Beaulieu Vineyard (outstanding wines, historic winery facility, excellent tour guides) then drive through St. Helena to Sterling Vineyards (beautiful winery, self-guided tour, and an air tram ride up and down the hill) just south of Calistoga.

After Sterling, go to Calistoga, walk around town, and have lunch. Then do a leisurely drive back downvalley, drive through St. Helena — stop for a little window shopping if you wish — and visit Robert Mondavi Winery just north of Oakville. Mondavi is perhaps the best known winery in the Napa Valley. The tour is optional; take it if you have time and are interested in yet another winery tour.

After Mondavi, continue south on Highway 29 to Yountville and visit shops in Vintage 1870 (40 shops in an historic building formerly a winery/distillery built in–yes–1870). Be sure to leave town by 3:30 or 4:00 to miss most of the traffic.

If you want to have dinner in the valley, stay in Yountville and cross Highway 29 on California Avenue at the south end of Yountville. Just before the entrance to the Veterans Home, turn right into Domaine Chandon. Chandon has an optional tour and excellent champagne. They're usually open till 6 p.m. They also have an outstanding restaurant. You may get lucky and find they have a table available for dinner.

After your pre-dinner champagne, go back into downtown Yountville and have dinner at one of the many outstanding restaurants in town. (Yountville probably has more good restaurants per capita than any town in California). By the time dinner is over, you can head home, secure in the knowledge that you've missed the traffic.

LET THE WINE SHUTTLE DRIVE

NAPA VALLEY WINE SHUTTLE

3031 California Blvd.
Napa, CA 94558
707.252.3135 • 800.258.8226

The Napa Valley Wine Shuttle drives between
a number of wineries and major hotels and B&Bs.
Their comfortable vehicles visit each stop every
30 minutes, so you can stay as long as you want
and sightsee at your own pace.

Cost is just $30 for the entire day (under 21 is
free) and there's no tasting charge at participating
wineries.

It's a great way to tour the valley.

SEEN IT ALL BEFORE?

If you've been there, done that, then you may be
interested in some of Napa Valley's little secrets.
We're sure that some of the locals here would just
as soon keep these favorites to themselves, but
we'll share them with you anyway. Just look for
the lock and key graphic next to the listings on
the following pages.

LOOK FOR THE "GRAPE CLUSTER"

We have awarded the coveted "Grape Cluster" to
exceptionally popular and well-known wineries,
restaurants, shops, and attractions. Each of the
awardees is an absolute favorite with us, and with
most first-time and repeat visitors. They are the
"best of the best" and very highly recommended.

THE "100 BEST"

These are the wineries, restaurants, sightseeing attractions, shops, recreational activities and hotels that we feel best represent the wide variety of experiences the Napa Valley has to offer. The 100 Best are listed alphabetically within each geographic area, and cities are listed from south to north. Listings on the Silverado Trail are at the end of the section.

AMERICAN CANYON

American Canyon is Napa County's newest and second largest city, incorporated in 1992. For those who drive north up Highway 80, it's the "gateway" to the Napa Valley.

NAPA-SONOMA WINE COUNTRY VISITORS CENTER
101 Antonina Drive
American Canyon CA 94589
707.642.0686 • 800.723.0575
Fax: 707.642.4610

Tourist information, wine tasting, delicatessen, light meals and souvenirs. They can also arrange for last-minute lodging. The Visitors Center is the first wine-related location for visitors coming from the East Bay. They have information on the *Sonoma* Valley too, but naturally we think you should visit *our* valley. It's still *the* place for wine and beauty.

NAPA

The City of Napa is the county seat and was founded in 1848 by Nathan Coombs. During Gold Rush days, cattle and lumber were mainstays of the local economy. Today the economy is based on wine and tourism; more than 60,000 people live here.

ALEXIS BAKING COMPANY & CAFE
1517 Third St.
Napa CA 94559
707.258.1827
Hours: 6:30 am - 7 pm Monday - Friday; 7:30 am - 8:00 pm Saturday. 8 am - 2 pm Sunday.

One of Napa's most popular coffee and lunch spots, "ABC" is now open most evenings for dinner. Highly recommended. For breakfast try their scrambled eggs with potatoes and tomato-basil toast. If you're lucky, they'll feature their grilled vegetable sandwich at lunchtime. Don't miss the unique, and uniquely labeled, bathrooms.

ANETTE'S CHOCOLATE & ICE CREAM FACTORY

1321 First Street
Napa CA 94559
707.252.4228

Ice cream fountain (they make more than 25 flavors), candy factory, wine-flavored truffles, sugar-free chocolates. They ship UPS almost everywhere. Anette took over from the previous owner, who'd founded the business 40 years earlier. The quality is still outstanding.

THE BEADED NOMAD

1238 First Street
Napa CA 94559
707.258.8004
Hours: Monday through Saturday 11 am - 6 pm; Sundays 12 - 5pm.

An incredible selection of beads of all sizes, shapes, colors and materials. Truly unique!

BISTRO DON GIOVANNI

4110 St. Helena Highway (Highway 29)
Napa CA 94558
707.224.3300

Overlooking Strack Vineyard and the hills beyond, Bistro Don Giovanni captures the essence of Italy with all the charm and elegance of the Napa Valley. Excellent menu featuring pizzas, pastas, grilled dishes (try the seared salmon with buttermilk), and exquisite salads (we like the spinach salad with Stilton cheese and fresh beets). We recommend the patio on a warm wine country evening, surrounded by the gardens that supply many of the herbs and vegetables for your meal. Ask for Dave, and be sure to try a "tomolive".

WHAT'S UP WITH THE CLOCK TOWER?

You'll know you're right downtown when you see the Clock Tower. Napans have mixed feelings about this thing. A minority actually like it. Many more (or at least they're more vocal) would be happy to tear it down with their hands and teeth. But everybody knows where it is. There's a fountain underneath it. It's not much better. But it's a convenient meeting place.

BRIDGEFORD FLYING SERVICES

Napa County Airport
Napa CA 94558
(Halfway between Napa and Vallejo)
707.224.0887

Tours of Napa Valley, Lake Berryessa, the Golden Gate Bridge and San
Francisco Bay, and the Marin and Sonoma Coasts. Cessna Skyhawk (1-3
passengers) or Cessna Centurion (4-5 passengers). Rates are $95 to $300 per
plane load depending on the number of passengers (up to 5) and type of tour.

A flying tour of the Napa Valley offers a truly unique and breathtaking
perspective of our enchanted valley. You realize just how much of the surrounding
area is still in its natural state. It's also the only way to see how the "other
half" lives (well, maybe much less than half). The hills on both sides of the
valley are filled with estates and compounds built by the wealthy. Most of
these stately homes are visible only from the air.

BUTTER CREAM BAKERY

2297 Jefferson Street
Napa CA 94558
707.255.6700

Try their "champagne cake". No, it doesn't have champagne in it. But it
deserves to accompany a glass of the bubbly. If you can't handle a whole cake,
you can buy it by the slice. Lots of other goodies, too; all with Butter Cream's
special touch. Truly a Napa institution and a popular hangout place for
breakfast or lunch. There's usually a line of people waiting to select their
favorite goodies from a wide variety of delicious pastries, so don't forget to
take a number when you walk in.

CARNEROS ALAMBIC DISTILLERY

1250 Cuttings Wharf Road
Napa CA 94559
707.253.9055
Hours: Spring/Summer open daily 10 am to 5 pm
Fall/Winter open Thursday through Monday 10:30 am to 4:30 pm
Cuttings Wharf Road is located off of Highway 12/121 between Napa and
Sonoma, approximately 5 miles southwest of downtown Napa.

An interesting tour, but unfortunately no tasting of their brandies and fine
liqueurs. However, their products are featured at Mustard's Grill in
Yountville, and the 25-year-old RMS makes an excellent after-dinner drink
to go along with a fine cigar.

CODORNIU NAPA

1345 Henry Road
Napa CA 94558
707.224.1668
Fax: 707.224.1672
Hours: Monday through Thursday from 10am to
5 pm, Friday through Sunday from 10 am to 3 pm
Tasting: $4.00 (no souvenir glass)

Go south from Napa to Highway 121 and turn
west toward Sonoma. Turn right on Old Sonoma
Road at Mont St. John Winery. Go one block,
then turn left on Dealy Lane. Proceed due west on
Dealy Lane, which becomes Henry Road where the
road curves beyond Carneros Creek Winery. Turn
left into Codorniu Napa's driveway. (Not easy, is
it? But it's worth the drive.)

In 1872, the Codorniu family of Barcelona
created the first *methode champenoise* sparkling
wine in Spain. 120 years later they came to the
Napa Valley to create a premium, distinctly
California, sparkling wine. Their winery, blending
into the surrounding landscape, is as beautiful
as their wine is delicious.

DOWNTOWN JOE'S

902 Main Street
Napa CA 94559
707.258.2337

Joe's represents the valley's fascination with the
fermentation process in all forms. Its beer can also
be found in other area restaurants that feature a
large beer list.

Joe's is a popular lunch, dinner and evening spot
for locals and those visitors who are lucky enough
to find out about it. Great food and, of course,
beer. It has live music almost every night and
"open mike" nights on Tuesday. Not the place for
a quiet, intimate dinner, but nice outdoor dining
where you can sit and look at the river.

EMBASSY SUITES

1075 California Boulevard
Napa CA 94559
707.253.9540 • 800.433.4600
Fax: 707.253.9202

A large and conveniently located inn just off Highway 29 (take the First Street exit). All 205 units are two-room suites, each with two phone lines with voice mail.

Suites face the indoor skylighted atrium, the outdoor pool, or the sun-drenched (and swan-inhabited) mill pond. There's also an indoor pool, spa, sauna and steam room. Guests enjoy a complimentary cooked-to-order American breakfast each morning, and an equally complimentary beverage reception each evening — with Napa Valley wine, of course. Rings in the courtyard serves from an Italian menu, and Joe's Bar offers live music and great drinks.

THE FLYING BOAR

4050 Byway East
Napa, California 94558
707.224.5904

This is one of Napa's most enjoyable restaurants. The Boar offers great food, comfortable surroundings, and a super friendly and helpful staff. It's open Tuesday - Thursday from 11:00 am - 9:00 pm and Friday and Saturday from 11:00 am - 9:30 pm. Try the Flying Boar burger, the grilled fresh fish of the day, or the Rib Eye steak with caramelized onions and gorgonzola.

To reach The Flying Boar, turn east off Highway 29 onto Trower, take the first left and the first left again (just past the John Muir Inn). Continue a short distance along the highway frontage road and you'll see the Boar on the right.

DEVA

1213 Coombs Street
Napa CA 94559
707.224.1397

Fragrantly funky, filled with the aroma of incense and oils. Owner Nancy Carter will be happy to talk with you for hours, and suggest which of her products (many of her own design and mixture) might please you best. Body oils, aromatherapy oils, greeting cards, posters, postcards, books, audiotapes, hanging things, psychic readings. It's small, loaded with stuff, and a very pleasant place to buy a gift for yourself or a loved one back home.

GENOVA DELICATESSEN

1550 Trancas Street
Napa CA 94558
707.253.8686

A wide selection of cheeses, meats and Italian specialties. They'll whip you up a sandwich or an entire picnic basket. If you can't find something here to delight your taste buds, you probably shouldn't have come to the Napa Valley in the first place.

HAKUSAN SAKE GARDENS

One Executive Way
Napa CA 94558
707.258.6160
Hours: 9 am to 6 pm
Complimentary tasting.
Directions: South of Napa on Highway 29 at the intersection of Highway 12. Entrance is off North Kelly Road.

Situated on 20 acres amid beautiful Japanese gardens. Constructed in 1989, Hakusan produces 180,000 cases of sake annually, using rice grown in the Sacramento Valley. A unique experience in the Napa Valley.

THE HESS COLLECTION WINERY

4411 Redwood Road
Napa CA 94558
707.255.1144
Hours: 10 am to 4 pm
Tasting: $2.50 without glass
Directions: Off Highway 29 in north Napa, turn west on Redwood Road (to the east this road is called Trancas Street). Stay on Redwood Road approximately 6.5 miles to the winery on the left, being careful to turn left over a bridge at the junction of Mount Veeder Road. Look for the sign on the bridge.

FOOTHILL CAFE

2766 Old Sonoma Road
Napa CA
707.252.6178

An out of the way place with tremendous food. Get grilled anything. Delicious. The San Francisco Chronicle says it's the equal of any restaurant in the Napa Valley. Many of us locals think it's even more than that.

THE JOY LUCK HOUSE

1144 Jordan Lane
Napa CA 94559
707.224.8788

Absolutely the best Chinese restaurant in Napa. In fact, it was voted the Best Asian Food in the Napa Valley by locals.

Featuring Hunan, Mandarin and Szechuan. Low fat with no MSG. Healthy and delicious.Be sure to check out the daily specials blackboard, and the Chef's Recommendations in the menu — they're always excellent!

The Hess Collection is both a winery and an art museum. Owner Donald Hess has assembled one of the largest modern art collections available for public viewing in California. This remarkable collection complements a winery that produces superb wines. Plus there's an excellent 12-minute audio-visual presentation on the winery. Highly recommended.

MARRIOTT NAPA VALLEY

3425 Solano Avenue
Napa CA 94558
707.253.7433
Fax 707.258.1320
Turn west on Redwood Road, cross the Wine Train tracks and turn right on Solano Avenue. Hotel is on left.

191 guest rooms, four suites, two restaurants. Heated outdoor pool and water spa. Lighted tennis courts. Fitness center. Training home of the Oakland Raiders football team. (They practice at Redwood Middle School just in back of the hotel).

NAPA PREMIUM OUTLETS

Highway 29 at First Street Exit
707.226.9876
Monday - Saturday 10 am - 8 pm.
Sundays 10 am - 6 pm

Includes Bass Clothing, Carole Little, Esprit, Gant, Geoffrey Beene, Izod, J. Crew, Liz Claiborne, Van Heusen, OshKosh B'Gosh, Timberland, Dansk, Mikasa, and Harry & David.

Brand new since 1995. Are they uniquely Napa Valley? No. Are they popular with tourists? You bet. That's why we've included them. And, if you get hungry, there are two great local restaurants, the Hunan (Chinese) and Fujiya (Japanese).

NAPA FIREFIGHTERS MUSEUM

1201 Main Street
Napa CA 94559
707.259.0609

Free admission. Open Friday, Saturday and Sunday 11 am to 4 pm.

Features hand pumper, hose carts, steamer, engines, ladder trucks, fire equipment and uniforms. A great place for kids!

NAPA VALLEY CONFERENCE AND VISITORS BUREAU

1310 Napa Town Center
Napa CA 94559
707.226.7459

Hidden in the Napa Town Center deep in the heart of downtown Napa, yet it gets tens of thousands of visitors a year. (Who knows how many people search but never find it? Many could still be driving the streets of Napa.) The CVB volunteers are outstanding; helpful, friendly and knowledgeable. Take advantage of their expertise to plan your valley destinations. (Even if you have this book, it can't hurt).

These people volunteer because they love talking with visitors. And they love the fact that they're wined and dined by the valley's best wineries and restaurants so that they'll have first-hand experience of the area's attractions. Most, but not all, are retired, so they have the time to help you and your fellow visitors enjoy their home.

Napa Valley Riverboat Company

PO Box 3677
Napa CA 94558
707.226.2628

Embarks from downtown Napa at the Main Street Landing, near the corner of Third Street and Main Street.Excursions (2 1/2 hours), Sunday brunch cruises (2 1/2 hours), sunset dinner cruise (3 hours), and charter trips.

The "City of Napa" is a sternwheeler originally called the "Bold Duck", brought from Portland to Napa in 1987. It includes a full galley, oak bar, fully upholstered perimeter seating, parquet dance floor, oak paneling and antique fixtures. It can accommodate up to 115 passengers and sails at a leisurely seven knots per hour.

Great fun. If you're obsessed with sternwheelers, or are visiting long enough to spend a truly leisurely several hours, come aboard. Great for kids, too. And, surprisingly for what is basically an "experience" rather than a restaurant, the food is excellent.

Napa Valley Traditions

1202 Main Street
Napa CA 94559
707.226.2044
Fax: 707.226.2069
Corner of Main and Pearl.

Traditions is a coffee house that also sells (and offers tastings of) food and wine. It specializes in Napa Valley products, including nuts, wine vinegars, olive oils, wine jellies, mustards and, of course, wines. Their Bayview Cellars offers Chardonnay, Gewurztraminer, Cabernet Sauvignon and Merlot. Lots of wine paraphernalia too, such as wine racks, coasters, cork pullers and the like.

Traditions is one of the original coffee hangouts in both Napa and California. It's a quiet and cool place to sip coffee or tea, with a play area for your little ones to occupy themselves while you relax. Traditions also happens to be just across the street from the Napa Firefighters Museum (previous page) which is *also* a great place to take kids.

NAPA VALLEY WINE TRAIN

1275 McKinstry
Napa CA 94559
707.253.2111• 800.427.4124
Fax: 707.253.9264

A 36-mile, three-hour brunch, lunch or dinner excursion through the heart of the Napa Valley. Meticulously restored 1917 Pullman Dining Car, damask linens, bone china, silver flatware, lead crystalware. Lounge and wine tasting cars are resplendent in polished mahogany, brass and etched glass. Wine Emporium stocks over 200 Napa Valley wines for purchase or shipping. Special "Winemaker Dinner" trips.

This is fun, folks. If you like trains, great food, great service and/or great views, take a trip. The whole thing is done with superb flair. If you think you'll be hungry soon, make sure you get the first seating. The second seating doesn't happen until one and a half hours later when the train starts its return trip from St. Helena–although you'll have hors d'oeuvres and beverages on the trip upvalley.

During your trip you may notice a few signs that seem to indicate that some of the locals don't care for the train. This is true. Some don't. The opponents are primarily "up-valley". They complain about the traffic that it allegedly produces, about the environmental damage, the noise, the danger at crossings; some have even alleged that the noise bothers their grapevines.

The Wine Train's opponents, although vocal, are probably greatly outnumbered by its proponents, and certainly by those who don't care one way or another. It's just a train. It's very pretty. It's a lot of fun to watch go by.

One of the creators of this book proposed to his wife on the Wine Train. It's definitely one of the more romantic spots (albeit a moving one) in the Napa Valley. Enjoy the trip.

THE NEIGHBORHOOD
An Antique Collective

1400 First Street
Napa CA 94559
707.258.0707

Located on Downtown Napa's main street, The Neighborhood represents sixty (that's right - 60!) different antique dealers from throughout the San Francisco Bay Area. Merchandise includes antique collectibles, new quality reproductions, and decorator pieces. The "Annex", at 1430 First Street, offers quality used furniture, glassware, giftware, and estate items. If you're an antique shopper or browser, you can't miss this place.

RED HEN ANTIQUES

5091 St. Helena Highway (Highway 29)
Napa CA 94558
707.257.0822
Open daily 10:00am -5:30pm
Oak Knoll Avenue west off Highway 29 between
Napa and Yountville

A unique and exciting collective of 70 antique
dealers set in a vineyard in the heart of the Napa
Valley. You could easily spend all day here.

PEARL

1339 Pearl Street #104
Napa CA 94559
707.224.9161
Fax: 707.255.6825
Open for lunch Tuesday
through Saturday.

Pearl co-owner Nickie
Zeller formerly
co-owned the legendary
Diner in Yountville,
and the Brown Street
Grill in Napa. She's
focusing her energies
now on Pearl, and it's
one of Napa's very best
restaurants.

RED ROCK CAFE AND CATERING

1010 Lincoln Avenue
Napa CA 94558
707.226.2633

Great hamburgers and onion rings. Barbecued ribs
too. Probably lots of other stuff but we've never
gotten past the burgers. Consistently voted the
best hamburger in Napa.

RIVERFRONT ANTIQUE CENTRE

705 Soscol Avenue
Napa CA 94559
707.253.1966
Open daily 10:00am -5:30pm

Over 24,000 square feet of antiques on the river in
downtown Napa. While you're in the neighborhood, check out the artists' studios and Feather
Fantasy, Napa Valley's biggest bird emporium.

SCIAMBRA-PASSINI FRENCH BAKERY

685 South Freeway Drive
Napa CA
707.252.3072

Tasty breads, cakes and pastries. Don't miss their
brick-oven baked sourdough and sweetdough
breads. Try it early in the morning or late in the
afternoon to get it fresh out of the oven.

SEGUIN MOREAU NAPA COOPERAGE

151 Camino Dorado
Napa CA 94558
707.252.3408

Just off Highway 29 south of Napa. Now —
how many places can you actually watch wine
barrels being made? A fascinating part of the wine
business that most visitors miss. A wonderful
educational experience for kids as they watch
skilled coopers plying their art in nearly the same
fashion as their ancestors have for hundreds of
years. Yes, kids, people still do this. And isn't that
neat the way they build a fire inside the barrel to
"toast" it?

SHACKFORD'S KITCHEN STORE

1350 Main Street
Napa CA 94559
707.226.2132

Open Monday thru Saturday, 9:30am to 5:30pm

Complete collection of cookware and cutlery,
kitchen accessories, baskets and gifts.

This place is absolutely loaded with kitchen stuff.
We always walk out with something, generally in
addition to what we came in for. It's the kind of
place every town used to have. Napa still has one.
And the staff is friendly and knowledgeable too.

SKYLINE WILDERNESS PARK

2201 Imola Avenue
Napa CA
707.252.0481
Hours: Monday-Thursday 9 am to dark
Friday-Sunday 8 am to dark

Skyline is an 850-acre wilderness area. It has over
25 miles of trails for hiking, biking and equestrian
use. The two-and-a-half mile main trail leads to
Lake Marie at the eastern end. There's also an

RIO POCO

807 Main Street
Napa CA 94559
707.253.8203

Delicious, down-home
real Mexican food in a
restaurant owned and
operated by a local
family. Mike and Donna
can be found in the
kitchen most every
night. If you are really
lucky, the special of the
day will be the rock
shrimp burrito. Also try
the vegetarian burrito.
Good prices too!

alternate route along the ridge trail which is a much better workout, but is not for those out of shape. From this trail on a clear day you can see San Francisco Bay, Mt. Tamalpais and Mt. Diablo. Beautiful.

Skyline also offers picnic and barbecue areas, an RV park, and tent camping. Daily visitor's fee is $4.00 per vehicle, RV camping $14.00, and tent sites $8.00. The best place to hike in Napa.

VALLERGA'S MARKET

3385 Solano Avenue
Napa CA 94558
707.253.2621

As good if not better than any other supermarket in the entire San Francisco Bay Area. Outstanding gourmet foods, perfect for picnic lunches. Vallerga's is also at two other locations in Napa (Silverado Trail and Imola Avenue), but this store just off Highway 29 at Redwood Road is the one you're most likely to be near.

YOUNTVILLE

In 1831 George Yount, the first American settler in the Napa Valley, came to the area now called Yountville. He received an 11,000 acre Mexican land grant and built the first structures in the area, a Kentucky blockhouse and mill. Even more importantly, he planted the first grapevines in the Napa Valley.

In 1855 Yount hired a surveyor to lay out a town site and named it "Sebastopol", ignoring the fact that a town in Sonoma County already had that name. In 1865, two years after his death, the town was renamed in his honor. His grave can be found in Pioneer Cemetery, next to Yountville Park at the north end of town.

When Yountville incorporated, it wanted to be called a "Village". The State of California didn't allow for villages, so Yountville had to refer to itself as a town. It still feels like a village, with a population of just over 3,000, half of those at the Veterans Home of California.

Yountville is a "walking town", filled with excellent shops, restaurants and lodging. Spend some time here. You'll enjoy it.

BRIX

7377 St. Helena Highway
Yountville, California
707-944-2749
Fax 707-944-8320

Napa Valley's hottest new spot. In addition to providing a distinctive dining experience, BRIX's wine market offers for sale a wide variety of Napa Valley wines and wine-related gifts. We hear they have the best wine list in the valley.

THE DINER

6476 Washington
Yountville CA 94599
707.944.2626
Legendary breakfasts. Delicious lunches. Fabulous dinners. A Napa Valley legend. Unfortunately it was long ago discovered by visitors so we have to share it. But you can still drop in without reservations and the quality has remained outstanding.

COMPADRE'S

6539 Washington Street
PO Box 3186
Yountville CA 94599
707.944.2406
Fax: 707.944.8407

Located between Vintage 1870 and the Vintage Inn.
Hours: Monday through Friday from 11 am,
Saturday and Sunday from 9 am.

Indoor and outdoor seating. Reservations not
required. Award-winning Mexican cuisine, with
traditional favorites complemented by an array of
grilled items, including fajitas, carnitas, and pollo
borracho, as well as fresh fish Vera Cruz style.
Wide range of appetizers, soups and salads, plus
outstanding burgers and desserts. "Compadres
400" selections feature items of 400 calories or
less. Large selection of vegetarian items. Imported
Mexican beers. Award-winning margaritas. Wines
available by glass or bottle. Wine list developed
with the help of local Napa Valley vintners.

If you're really brave, try the "Wall of Flame":
a selection of over 100 hot sauces for your sampling
pleasure. For first aid, wash it all down with a
frozen margarita.

DOMAINE CHANDON WINERY & RESTAURANT

1 California Drive
Yountville CA 94599
707.944.2280
Hours: May through October — 11 am to 6 pm;
November through April — Wednesday through
Sunday: 11 am to 6 pm
Directions: West side of Highway 29 (at Yountville).
Take the Veterans Home exit. Cross railroad tracks
and turn right into Domaine Chandon.

Domaine Chandon is owned by Moet et Chandon,
and its sparkling wines are superb. It also offers an
excellent tour, giving you a chance to see how

sparkling wines are made, which is a quite different process from the "still" wines made in most other Napa Valley wineries. Charge for tasting.

The restaurant is open for luncheon from 11:30 am to 2:30 pm, and dinner from 6:00 pm. Reservations are advised — telephone: 707.944.2892 (between 10 am and 5 pm). Closed for dinner on Mondays and Tuesdays year-round. November through April — closed all day Monday and Tuesday.

Domaine Chandon's restaurant is one of the most outstanding in the valley. The food, presentation, service and views are superb. Unless you're very lucky, you'll need reservations well in advance.

FRENCH LAUNDRY RESTAURANT

6640 Washington
Yountville CA 94599
707.944.2380

There's no sign out front so you're unlikely to even spot the place unless you already know it's there. You probably can't even get a reservation for at least six months — at best. But, hey, why not? Give them a call. Every once in a while they actually get a cancellation and the vacancy could be yours. (You'll find the "Laundry" also mentioned in our *Plan Ahead* section. Reservations got even harder this year when Chef Thomas Keller was named the top chef in America by the James Beard Foundation)

HOT AIR BALLOONS

Hot air ballooning is something you have to experience to truly appreciate. Drifting almost soundlessly over the hills and vineyards of the valley, you'll come to experience the breathtaking beauty of this famous part of the world.

Most balloons launch from the Yountville area early in the morning. The first "shift" rides in the balloon gondola while the second shift pursues the balloon in the "chase" vehicle. Then, after the balloon sets down at the end of its voyage, the two

Veterans Home

The Veterans Home of California opened in 1884. It's open to anyone from California who served in the military and currently has over 1400 residents. The grounds are open to the public; feel free to wander around. You also might want to visit the museum near the entrance. The Napa Valley Symphony performs in the home's Lincoln Hall, and Fourth of July fireworks are held here every year. In fact, they're probably the most popular place in the valley for such fireworks.

crews switch for the second flight. Almost every morning's flight ends in a champagne brunch. You can even get married in a balloon. Cost, including brunch, ranges from $150-$175 per person for a one-hour flight.

Adventures Aloft
800.944.4408 • 707.944.4408

Balloons Above the Valley
800.464.6824

Balloon Aviation of Napa Valley
800.367.6272 • 707.944.4400

Bonaventura Balloon Company
800.359.6272 • 707.944.2822

Napa Valley Balloons Inc.
800.253.2224 • 707.944.0228

McAllister Water Gardens

7420 St. Helena Highway
Yountville CA 94599
707.944.0921

March through September
Thursday-Sunday 9 am - 4 pm

Discover tranquillity and peace among the water lilies, pond plants and goldfish. An interesting place to visit and a great place to buy water life for your home. They'll even ship.

Mustard's Grill

73399 St. Helena Highway (Highway 29)
Yountville CA 94599
707.944.2424

One of the most popular restaurants in the Napa Valley. And one of the best. If you try the Mongolian pork chops, you might end up asking for them every time. However, if it's within your price range, try the filet mignon; it's pure manna from heaven and simply melts in your mouth.

Mustard's prides itself on its outrageously comprehensive wine list — nearly 400 wines at last count — and the highly professional staff is well educated and able to advise you on an appropriate wine for your meal. Mustard's is truly a dining experience.

NAPA VALLEY GRILLE

6795 Washington Street (in Washington Square)
Yountville CA 94599
707.944.8686

The Grille, just off Highway 29 and Madison, is one of Yountville's and the valley's favorite places. Excellent food, outdoor dining with a great view of vineyards and hills, and a wide variety of seating choices, including intimate one-table rooms in "The Gallery".

Executive Chef Bob Hurley has created a deliciously international menu, with an emphasis on Mediterranean and California cuisine. Not surprising, since his history includes Auberge du Soleil, Masa's, Star's, and Domaine Chandon. Highly recommended.

PIATTI RISTORANTE

6480 Washington
Yountville CA 94599
707.944.2070

A favorite of locals and visitors. A focus on light, moderately priced meals. Comfortable and enjoyable. Outdoor dining, too.

VERANDA CLUB SPA

Washington Square
Yountville
707.944.1906 Fax: 707.944.0766

The Veranda Club Spa was established in 1987 as *Massage Werkes* by proprietor Wil Anderson.

Wil has practiced and taught in Germany and Switzerland, and is a specialist in a variety of massage techniques, including the esoteric and remarkably effective deep body massage called *Chua Ka*.

The spa offers massage, facials, body treatments, and total fitness programs. It's one of those intimate little places that make the Napa Valley so special, and it's very popular with those who want the personal attention that larger spas can't provide. If you're staying at one of the inns or B&Bs in Yountville, you can walk here in minutes. Spoil yourself. After all, you're on vacation.

VINTAGE INN
6541 Washington Street
Yountville CA 94599
707.944.1112

A beautifully designed (by the same architect who did the spectacular Ventana Inn at Big Sur) and landscaped inn in the heart of Yountville. This used to be an old-growth vineyard with gnarly old vines just across the street from the home of one of the creators of this book. If the vineyard had to go — and there was no preventing it — there could be no better development to replace it than the Vintage Inn. An excellent place to stay and relax.

VINTAGE 1870
6525 Washington Street
Yountville CA 94599
707.944.2451
Fax: 707.944.2453
Hours: Daily 10 am to 5:30 pm

Listed in the National Registry of Historic Places, Vintage 1870 was built as a distillery and winery by Gottlieb Groezinger in 1870. Today it offers more than 40 specialty shops, wine tasting at the Wine Cellar, restaurants and a picnic garden.

One of our favorite shops is the Toy Cellar for kids of all ages. Vintage 1870 is probably the most popular place for tourists to shop in the entire Napa Valley.

YOUNTVILLE PARK

On Washington Street at the north end of Yountville just across the street from the Napa Valley Lodge.

A very popular place for picnics and one of the best parks around for kids, boasting a unique assortment of play equipment. Across the street from the park is Pioneer Cemetery and the grave of George Yount, first settler in the valley and the founder of Yountville.

When Yount first saw the valley in 1831, he said: "In such a place I would like to live and die." He did, dying in 1865.

OAKVILLE

POMETTA'S DELICATESSEN AND CATERING

7787 Highway 29 (at Oakville Grade)
Oakville CA 94562
707.944.2365

An unincorporated area with a great little post office. Famous for its grocery store and surrounding wineries.

Picnic lunches to go, specialty sandwiches, catering, outdoor seating. Try the barbecue chicken sandwich (actually roasted, with herbs, and delicious). Call in advance and they'll have your order ready. You can even take a break with a game of horseshoes.

THE OAKVILLE GROCERY

7856 Saint Helena Highway (Highway 29)
Oakville CA 94562
707.944.8802
Fax: 707.944.1844

The Grocery's building opened as a general store in 1880 and it's in the National Registry of Historic Places. The Grocery has been featured on national TV shows and in major food and wine publications as one of the best specialty food stores in the country. Grocery, charcuterie, fresh foods, cheese, olives, gift baskets, wines, espresso, baked goods, sandwiches and they'll ship anywhere.

ROBERT MONDAVI WINERY

7801 St. Helena Highway (Highway 29)
Oakville CA 94562
800.MONDAVI
Hours: May through October — 9 am to 5:30 pm
November through April — 9:30 am to 4:30 pm
On the west side of Highway 29, just 1/2 mile north of Oakville.

Complimentary tasting

The place that rekindled the Napa Valley wine industry. Opened in 1966, it was the first winery built in the valley after Prohibition (that weird "experiment" when America decided it didn't want to let its citizens drink alcohol). Founder Robert Mondavi has a well deserved reputation as a wine-making icon and his publics relation efforts have benefited every winery in the valley.

The winery offers beautiful Spanish-mission style architecture, excellent tours, wonderful wines, frequent art shows and its famous annual Mondavi Summer Music Festival.

If you've never before visited the valley, this is a *must* stop. Even if you're a frequent visitor, you'll want to stop by again and again. Don't miss the beautiful Benjamin Bufano statue of St. Francis at the main entrance.

BEAULIEU VINEYARD

1960 St. Helena Highway (Highway 29)
Rutherford CA 94573
707.963-2411
Hours: Tours from 10 am to 3 pm,
tastings from 10 am to 4 pm

Another unincorporated town best known for its two major wineries on Highway 29 — Beaulieu and Niebaum-Coppola (formerly Inglenook).

Complimentary tasting. Charge for vintage wines.

For many locals and wine aficionados, Napa Valley wineries can be divided into two categories: Beaulieu Vineyard, and all the others. BV was winning awards world wide when most other current Napa Valley vineyards were still planted with prunes. The winery was founded in 1900 by Georges de Latour and survived Prohibition by producing sacramental wines. BV's wines have been served by every president of the United States since Franklin Roosevelt.

A beautiful visitors' center offers outstanding complimentary wines and tours by friendly, very knowledgeable guides. The redwood vats and aging areas smell like a winery is supposed to smell — musky, winey, and absolutely enticing. A *must* for your first visit to the valley. And a "let's just stop in for a glass or two" for repeat visits.

NIEBAUM-COPPOLA ESTATE WINERY

1991 St. Helena Highway
Rutherford CA 94573
707.963.9099
Hours: 10 am - 5 pm
Tours by appointment

In 1995, owner Francis Ford Coppola ("The Godfather", "Apocalypse Now") and his wife Eleanor expanded their wine estate with the purchase of the former Inglenook Winery, which dates back to 1879. The chateau and grounds include a museum of wine and film. A visit gives you both excellent wine and the opportunity to see Oscars won by Coppola, a Tucker automobile from his movie "Tucker", the boat from "Apocalypse Now", photos and other memorabilia.

RUTHERFORD GRILL

1180 Rutherford Road
Rutherford CA
707.963.1792

A fun, but often very noisy, place. Excellent and varied menu suitable for both kids and adults. And with all the noise, nobody's going to care about a little kid noise. Right next to Beaulieu Vineyard, so you can sip great wine before lunch. Or after.

ST. SUPÉRY VINEYARD & WINERY

8440 St. Helena Highway
Rutherford CA 94573
707.963.4507 • 800.942.0809
Hours: Daily 9:30am - 4:30pm
Nominal tasting charge
Located on east side of Highway 29 between Oakville and Rutherford

St. Supéry's Wine Discovery Center offers guided tours throughout the day. Tours include the display vineyard, where you can wander among the vines, taste the grapes and take photographs. Meticulously designed exhibits explain the making of fine wines from soil to bottle. The tour ends with a conducted tasting of St. Supéry wines.

A highlight of the tour is "SmellaVision", which includes two exhibits, one for Sauvignon Blanc (a white wine) and one for Cabernet Sauvignon (a red). Each stand displays four bottles of the specific varietal so you can see that even within a Sauvignon Blanc or Cabernet Sauvignon there are often great variations in color, clarity and appearance.

The "smell" part of the exhibits comes into play when you push any one of the four levers at each stand, put your nose over a long plexiglass "sniffer tube" and get a whiff of one of the many aromas which are often used in describing these wines.

At the wine tasting that follows the tour, you're ready to search for these aromas in a real glass of wine.

ST. HELENA

BALE GRIST MILL STATE HISTORIC PARK

3369 North Saint Helena Highway (Highway 29)
St. Helena CA 94574
707.963.2236
Three miles north of St. Helena
Hours 10 am to 5 pm

Open throughout the year. Built in 1846, the mill has been restored to operating condition complete with its 36-foot wooden waterwheel and big millstones. On weekends, you can watch the mill in action, grinding grain to produce stone ground flour. A fun and educational experience for the kids — and parents, too.

Founded in 1853 and the high-profile center of the Napa Valley wine industry. It's still a small town with less than 6,000 people. The main street of St. Helena is, coincidentally, called Main Street. (It's also Highway 29 and the St. Helena Highway). Main Street is loaded with enough boutiques to sink a boatload of yuppies. Enjoy yourself. It's smalltown America with a designer's touch.

BERINGER VINEYARDS

1000 Pratt Avenue
St. Helena CA 94574
707.963.4812
Hours: 10-6 summer (last tour at 5), 9:30-5 winter (last tour at 4)
Complimentary tasting

Built in 1876, the winery has been operating continuously ever since. The famous "Rhine House" contains the visitors center. This classic Napa Valley winery is a good place to stop for a photograph.

BRAVA TERRACE

3010 St. Helena Highway North (at Lodi Lane)
St. Helena CA 94574
707.963.9300
Fax 707-963-9581

Superb food. Another one (there are an awful lot) of the outstanding restaurants in the valley. A rainy night in the valley (yes, it happens) cries out for a bowl of their French onion soup, a loaf of bread and a bottle of Merlot from the adjacent Freemark Abbey Winery.

Not only are kids welcome, but you can get your order to go.

THE CULINARY INSTITUTE OF AMERICA AT GREYSTONE
WINE SPECTATOR GREYSTONE RESTAURANT

2555 Main Street
St. Helena CA 94574
707.963.1100

Formerly Christian Brothers Winery. Literally filled with kitchens and dining areas. The West Coast branch of the renowned cooking school with a restaurant open to the public. A majestic building that's a favorite for photographers, which is why we've given it our Grape Cluster Award.

EL BONITA MOTEL

195 Main Street.
St. Helena CA 94574
707.963.3216

El Bonita looks like an art-deco motel, but it's much, much more. It's a charming, comfortable, and reasonably priced place to stay, with 2 1/2 acres of beautifully landscaped gardens. It's where St. Helena residents suggest that their friends stay when they come to the valley.

ANA'S CANTINA

1205 Main Street
707-963-4921
You won't see this one in the tourist guides, but it's a favorite local hangout with pool, and good beer on tap.

GIUGNI & SON GROCERY COMPANY

1227 Main Street
St. Helena CA 94574
707.963.3421

Cheapest, best, most humongous sandwiches in
town. An institution for years.

HURD BEESWAX CANDLES

3020 North St. Helena Highway (Highway 29)
St. Helena CA 94574
707.963.7211

A wonderful place for gifts for friends, family and
even yourself. Candles in all sizes, styles, colors
and shapes.

CHARLES KRUG WINERY

2800 St. Helena Highway
St. Helena CA 94574
Daily 10:30 - 5:30
707.967.2201
Tours 11:30am, 1:30pm and 3:30pm daily except
Wednesday.
Charge for tasting except Wednesday.

Founded in 1861, Krug is the oldest operating
winery in the Napa Valley, so it deserves our
Grape Cluster Award. Location of a number of
musical and theatrical events.

LOUIS M. MARTINI WINERY

254 South St. Helena Highway (Highway 29)
St. Helena CA 94574
707.963.2736 • 800.321.9463
Hours: Daily 10-4:30
Complimentary tasting, charge for reserve wines

The oldest family-owned winery in the valley, in
operation since 1933. That qualifies it for our Grape
Cluster Award. Excellent wine, great tour guides.

GILLWOOD'S RESTAURANT

1313 Main Street
St. Helena CA 94574
707.963.1788

Popular local hangout
with a community
table where solo diners
can have mealtime
company.

45

NAPA VALLEY COFFEE ROASTING COMPANY

1400 Oak Avenue
St. Helena CA 94574
707.963.4491 • 800.852.5805
Fax: 707.963.1183

There's one of these in Napa, too, but this one has lots more room and outdoor seating. Great coffee. Great atmosphere. Adjacent to Tantau (another "100 Best" } and close to many of the Main Street shops such as Vanderbilt and Company, this is the place to start your morning of shopping in St. Helena.

SPRING STREET RESTAURANT

1245 Spring
St. Helena CA 94574
707.963.5578
Great food. Indoor and outdoor dining. A very popular place for locals throughout the valley.

NAPA VALLEY MUSEUM

473 Main Street
St. Helena, CA 94574
707.963.7411

Hours: Monday through Friday, 9:00am-4:00pm
Saturday & Sunday, 11:00am-3:00pm

The museum is devoted to the history of the Napa Valley and the people who have lived here. There are exhibits on the environment, Wappo Indians, Spanish missionaries, Mexican ranchos, Yankee settlers, long-since disappeared railroads and hot spring resorts, and of course the wine industry. The museum will be moving to a permanent location at the Veterans Home in Yountville, probably in 1998. But you don't have to wait till then to enjoy it.

NAPA VALLEY OLIVE OIL MANUFACTURING CO.

835 Charter Oak Avenue
St. Helena CA 94574
707.963.4173

A favorite of locals and visitors. Quite out of the way, so you're unlikely to stumble on it unless someone gives you a hint. Great cheeses and other Italian goodies. And tremendous (and economical) olive oil by the jug, made by the owners themselves.

PRAGER PORTS AND WINES

1281 Lewelling
St. Helena CA 94574
707.963.7678
Between Sutter Home Winery and Harvest Inn
Hours: 10:30-4:30. Tasting fee: $3.00 redeemable toward wine purchase.

A small, family-owned winery whose ports and wines are sold only at the winery. Prager also has a two-suite B & B, one suite over the winery, the other in the vineyards.

SHOWLEY'S AT MIRAMONTE

1327 Railroad Avenue
St. Helena CA 94574
707.963.1200
Fax: 707.963.8864

A medium-priced meal but first-class atmosphere and excellent food. Friday night jazz.

SILVERADO MUSEUM

PO Box 409
1490 Library Lane
St. Helena CA 94574
707.963.3757
Fax: 707.963.0917
Open daily except Monday and holidays from noon to 4 p.m. Free admission.

Devoted to Robert Louis Stevenson, the author of such classics as *Treasure Island, Dr. Jekyll and Mr. Hyde* and *A Child's Garden of Verses.* In 1880, Stevenson spent his honeymoon in an abandoned bunkhouse at the old Silverado Mine on the slope of Mount St. Helena. *The Silverado Squatters* is his account of his stay there.

THE SPOT

587 South Saint Helena Highway (Highway 29)
St. Helena CA 94574
707.963.2844

Hamburgers, hot dogs, pizzas, milk shakes at their full-serve soda fountain. Decor is straight out of the 50's. A wonderful place for the family. Naturally it's a favorite of the locals.

The museum works at all levels, for eager
six-year-olds as well as bibliophiles and scholars.
Includes original letters, manuscripts, first
and variant editions, paintings, sculptures,
photographs and memorabilia.

ST. HELENA PREMIUM OUTLETS

Highway 29 North, 2 miles past St. Helena
707.963.7282
Daily 10 am - 6 pm

Includes Donna Karan, Brooks Brothers, Joan &
David, and London Fog

SPIRITS IN STONE

Village Outlets, Suite 2D
3111 Saint Helena Highway
St. Helena CA 94574
707.963.7000 • 800.974.6629

Contemporary Zimbabwe Shona sculpture.
Newsweek says, "Perhaps the most important new
art form to emerge from Africa in this century."
The gallery's brochure says, "Sculpting with
simple tools, the self-taught artists carve stones
that illumine with more than 200 color variations.
A diverse body of work with dynamic, spiritual
themes." We say, "This stuff is absolutely
beautiful."

SUTTER HOME WINERY

277 St. Helena Highway South (Highway 29)
St. Helena CA 94574
707.963.3104
Hours: 9 am to 5 pm
Directions: At south end of St. Helena on west
side of Highway 29 (across from Louis Martini
Winery). Approximately 3.5 miles north of
Rutherford.

The House of White Zin. Originally a small
family winery, their invention of White Zinfandel

made them a fortune — and the largest winery in the Napa Valley. Tours and complimentary wine tasting. If you've ever enjoyed a glass of White Zin, you owe it to yourself to stop by Sutter Home, have another, and thank them.

Yes, there is a "Red Zin" and has been for many years. In fact, that's what true Zinfandel is. Zinfandel is not a white grape, it's red. (Of course red wines actually come from black grapes and real white wines come from green grapes, but that's another story). White Zinfandel is made by removing the wine from contact with the grape skins very early in the fermentation process, so that very little color is extracted. The result is a whitish wine that's usually served cold and definitely very popular.

TANTAU

1220 Adams Street
St. Helena CA 94574
707.963.3115

A gallery and gift shop owned by a mother-daughter team with a whimsical eye for the unique and beautiful. Sally and Margot's shop is filled with wonderful things for the home, including antiques, new furniture, one-of-a-kind art pieces, pottery, linens, frames, lamps, stationery, and a wide variety of accessories and gifts.

TRA VIGNE RESTAURANT

1050 Charter Oak Avenue
St. Helena CA 94574
707.963.4444

Many consider this to be the best restaurant in the Napa Valley. No one denies that it's right up there among the very finest. It's a great place in which to hang out, munching on the marinated olives they serve at the bar.

V. Sattui Winery

1111 White Lane
St. Helena CA 94574
707.963.7774 • Fax: 707.963.4324
Open daily 9 am to 6 pm (5 pm, Nov. to Feb.)
Complimentary tasting
Just 1 1/2 miles south of St. Helena along the
east side of Highway 29 across from the Beacon
gas station. To avoid a parking ticket, park in
the winery parking lot, not on White Lane.

Some wineries have mumbled about Sattui being
a retail shop rather than a winery (overlooking how
many things they sell in their own retail shops). The
reality is that Darryl Sattui does a very good job at
both winemaking and retailing. Visitors love it. The
award-winning wine is excellent and complimentary.
(And it's not available anywhere but the winery.)
The gourmet deli offers over 200 different cheeses.
And visitors can enjoy lunch in the two-acre shaded
picnic area. Highly recommended.

White Sulphur Springs Retreat & Conference Center

3100 White Sulphur Springs Road
St. Helena CA 94574
707.963.8588 • Fax: 707.963.2890
Directions: In St. Helena, turn west on Spring St.
at the Exxon gas station. Go 3 miles to end of road.

White Sulphur Springs was California's first hot
springs resort. Its natural beauty has been retained
since the resort was founded in 1852. Nestled in
a canyon just west of St. Helena, the resort offers
seclusion and tranquillity. Hiking trails lead through
mature redwood, madrone and fir trees, over
meandering creeks and around cascading waterfalls.

Creekside Cottages provide a private and comfortable
setting. The Inn has rooms with rustic charm. The
Carriage House offers cozy rooms with shared baths
and a inviting hospitality lounge. Sulphur soaking
pool, sauna, whirlpool bath. Rates from $70-$145.

CALISTOGA

Calistoga was developed in the 1860's and its name is reputed to have been accidentally coined by town founder Sam Brannan. Brannan apparently intended to refer to it as the "Saratoga of California", the "Saratoga" referring to the well-known spa area in New York State. Brannan, having had a few drinks, instead came out with the "Calistoga of Sarafornia". Calistoga it stayed.

Calistoga is *the* place for spas, and it's the only town in the Napa Valley with any real nightlife — despite the fact that it has only one-tenth the population of the city of Napa. People walk along the sidewalks; wander in and out of bars, restaurants and shops; smile at each other; and, in general, have a great time. After all, after lying in mud, soaking in bubbling mineral water and getting massaged throughout the day, you'd be pretty mellow, too.

ALL SEASONS CAFE

1400 Lincoln Avenue
Calistoga CA 94515
707.942.9111
Legendary, with a killer wine list. Great vegetarian fare and "to die for" desserts.

BOTHE-NAPA VALLEY STATE PARK

3801 North Saint Helena Highway (Highway 29)
Calistoga CA 94515
707.942.4575

Excellent trails through beautiful redwood groves. Picnic and camping areas. Outdoor swimming pool. A wonderful place for all ages. We've given the park our Grape Cluster Award because it's the loveliest public place to hike in the entire valley.

CALISTOGA GLIDERPORT

1546 Lincoln Avenue
Calistoga CA 94515
707.942.5000

One- and two-passenger rides:
one person -$79/20 minutes & $110/30 minutes.
two person - $110/20 minutes & $150/30 minutes.
Biplane rides:
one person - $95/20 minutes & $120/30 minutes.
two person - $120/20 minutes & $160/30 minutes.

Nothing, absolutely nothing, is like the whispering silence of a glider as you sail over the vineyards and hills of the Napa Valley.

CALISTOGA INN & RESTAURANT

1250 Lincoln Avenue
Calistoga CA 94515
707.942.4101

Another long-time favorite of locals and visitors. Live, local musicians on the weekends and dynamite buffalo wings. It also has its own excellent microbrewery.

CALISTOGA MINERAL WATER COMPANY

865 Silverado Trail North
Calistoga CA 94515
707.942.6295

Visitors are very welcome. Come see where this "designer water" actually comes from. Take a tour and enjoy a water tasting with lots of different flavors. Due to government regulations the company can't advertise its water as healthful, but the reality is they've got lots of testimonials and people have been drinking (and bathing in) Calistoga's water for more than a hundred years as a health tonic.

CLOS PEGASE WINERY

1060 Dunaweal Lane
Calistoga CA 94515
707.942.4981
Hours: 10:30 am to 5 pm
Tasting:$2.50
Guided tours at 11:00 am & 2:00 pm.
Reservations appreciated.
Directions: 7 miles north of St. Helena to Dunaweal
Lane and turn right. 1/2 mile to winery on the left.

Clos Pegase is named after Pegasus, the winged
horse of Greek mythology. According to legend,
the birth of both wine and art occurred when
Pegasus' hooves unleashed the sacred Spring of
the Muses.

After an international competition, the winery
was designed by renowned architect Michael
Graves, who was commissioned to build a "temple
to wine". The architecture is absolutely stunning.
It's a rather amazing place for a picnic, which you
can do in the company of a 300-year-old oak tree
and adjacent Merlot vineyard.

On the third Saturday of each month (except
December & January), owner Jan Shrem's slide
presentation, "Wine Seen Through 4,000 Years of
Health, Literature, History and Art," is presented
free to the public.

INDIAN SPRINGS RESORT

1712 Lincoln Avenue
Calistoga CA 94515
707.942.4913 • Fax: 707.942.4919

The oldest continuously operating thermal pool
and spa facility in California. Situated on three
thermal geysers and 16 acres of ancient volcanic
ash. The 1913 bath house has been restored to
pristine condition. Ceiling fans circulate the air,
thermal geysers warm the volcanic ash in the mud
baths and sterilize the mud after each use, gentle
music is piped throughout the treatment rooms,
and mineral water fragrant with fresh citrus and

WAPPO BAR & BISTRO
1226 Washington St.
Calistoga CA 94515
707.942.4712

Upscale. Locals and visitors rave about the food and its presentation.

cucumber is provided by the well trained and solicitous staff throughout the treatment.

Mud baths, mineral baths, massages, Remy Laure facial and body polish treatments. Large mineral pool.

MOUNT VIEW HOTEL & SPA
1457 Lincoln Avenue
Calistoga CA 94515
707.942.5789 • 800.772.8838
Fax: 707.942.9165

An inviting health spa featuring a pool, natural mineral water, Jacuzzi, poolside dining, Swedish massage, aromatherapy massage, sports massage, shiatsu massage, reflexology, whirlpool baths, body wraps (herbal, mud, seaweed, and valerian) and facials.

Renowned chef Jan Birbaum's Catahoula Restaurant & Saloon serves up the best Cajun food in Northern California.

OLD FAITHFUL GEYSER OF CALIFORNIA
1299 Tubbs Lane
Calistoga CA 94515
707.942.6463 • Fax: 707.942.6898
Open daily at 9 am
$5 adults, $2 children 6-12.

One of only three Old Faithful geysers in the world, erupting approximately every 40 minutes and shooting water 60 feet into the air.

A scientific study sponsored by the Carnegie Institute's Department of Terrestrial Magnetism is currently being conducted here in order to document the possible correlation between the geyser's eruptions and earthquake activity.

Geothermal exhibit hall, gift shop, picnic area and self-guided geothermal tour. Private moonlight parties for 20 or more by reservation only.

PETRIFIED FOREST

4100 Petrified Forest Road
Calistoga CA 94515
707.942.6667
Open daily 10-5
Six miles west of Calistoga.
$3 adults, $1 children.

A fascinating and educational example of the
powers of nature and the vastness of time. Huge
petrified trees scattered throughout the grounds as
well as a museum and gift shop. Excellent for
older kids.

ROBERT LOUIS STEVENSON STATE PARK

3801 North St. Helena Highway
Calistoga CA 94515
707.942.4575

Open during daylight hours. Hiking trail to the
top of Mount St. Helena. Bring your own drinking
water for the long, sometimes very hot, climb up
the mountain. Best time to visit is spring or fall.
The view from the summit includes the nearby
geyser country and, weather permitting, distant
mountains such as Lassen, Shasta and the Sierra
Nevada. No restrooms.

SHARPSTEEN MUSEUM

1311 Washington Street
Calistoga CA 94515
707.942.5911
One block west of Lincoln Ave. on Washington St.
Hours: 10 am - 4 pm, April - October
Noon - 4 pm., November - March
Free admission.

Sweeping dioramas, fascinating artifacts and
unusual exhibits in a museum created by Ben
Sharpsteen, Walt Disney Studio animator and
Oscar-winning producer.

GOLDEN HAVEN SPA

Hot Springs Resort
1713 Lake Street
Calistoga CA 94515
707.942.6793

Off the beaten path, this
inexpensive motel is
located three blocks from
Calistoga's main street.
Open to the public 9 am
to 9 pm, a favorite for
mud baths, whirlpools,
blanket wraps, mineral
baths, massage, foot
reflexology, swimming
pool and hot mineral
pool. It's not as fancy as
the others, but it is one of
the few places in
Calistoga where a couple
can enjoy a mud bath
together.

Exhibits include: A 32 foot-long diorama depicting 1860s life at the opulent resort that gave Calistoga– "the Saratoga of the Pacific"–its name. An elaborately furnished cottage from the lavish Victorian spa resort. A restored stagecoach that encountered many a bandit on its mountain journeys. A working model of an 1871 train. Vintage car memorabilia. A Native American exhibit. A Robert Louis Stevenson exhibit and bronze sculpture.

STERLING VINEYARDS

1111 Dunaweal Lane
Calistoga CA 94515
707.942.3344
Hours: 10:30 am to 4:30 pm
North of St. Helena turn east on Dunaweal Lane
Sky Tram: $6.00 includes tasting. ($3.00 under 18)

A beautiful Moorish-style winery, sparkling white on top of a hill just south of Calistoga. Travel the Sky Tram to the winery where you can take a leisurely self-paced tour. Gorgeous views of the valley below.

DR. WILKINSON'S HOT SPRINGS

1507 Lincoln Avenue
Calistoga CA 94515
707.942.4102
Located at the corner of Lincoln and Fairway in the heart of Calistoga

Mud baths, massage, mineral baths, facials, acupressure facelifts, salt glow scrubs, Terra-Thalasso body treatment, and cerofango treatments (a unique application of mud, clay, botanicals and paraffin to the hands and feet). Indoor and outdoor pools, comfortable lodging.

For nearly 50 years, Dr. Wilkinson has offered visitors the soothing, invigorating magic of his mud treatments. Some people say just mentioning Doc's name can relieve stress and relax the soul.

ANGWIN

PACIFIC UNION COLLEGE

Angwin CA 94508
800.862.7080 • Fax: 707.965.6390

With a student body of 1,500 and a student-teacher ratio of 13:1, this Seventh Day Adventist college is rated one of the top liberal arts colleges in the West. Example: It's one of the top 10 schools in the nation whose graduates are accepted into medical school. PUC's 200-acre campus is surrounded by 1,800 acres of agricultural and forested land—a great hiking area.

Nestled at the top of Howell Mountain, overlooking the Napa Valley, is the quiet college community of Angwin.

Right accross from the college is a small shopping center with a post office, and a huge vegetarian grocery store. Both are closed Saturdays.

LAKE BERRYESSA

SPANISH FLAT RESORT

4290 Knoxville Road
Napa CA 94558
707.966.7700

Complete marina facilities. Power boats, boat ramp, jet ski rental, open and covered berths, secure boat garages, gas, fishing boats, supplies. Less than one mile from grocery store, deli, sporting goods, beauty shop, post office, service station, restaurant and bar.

A popular launching point for fishermen. A wide variety of fish can be found in the lake, including bass, rainbow trout, brown trout, bluegill, crappe, and catfish.

Prior to 1957, Lake Berryessa was Monticello Valley and the town of Monticello. When Monticello Dam was completed, the lake started filling. Today it is one of the largest manmade lakes in California, 25 miles long, 3 miles wide and 275 feet deep at its deepest point, with 168 miles of shoreline.

Campgrounds and picnic areas are abundant.

SILVERADO TRAIL

MUMM NAPA VALLEY

8445 Silverado Trail
Rutherford CA 94573
707.942.3434 • Fax: 707.942.3470
Hours: 10:30 am to 6 pm; 10 am to 5 pm - November 1 to April 1. Complimentary tours on the hour from 11-4 (no 4 o'clock tour in winter). Tasting $3.50 and up

The Silverado Trail runs along the east side of the valley from Calistoga at the northern end to Napa at the southern end. There are many more wineries along the Trail than the few we've listed here.

On west side of Silverado Trail, approximately 2 miles north of Oakville Cross Road

The *Wine Spectator* has called Mumm Napa Valley "perhaps the best sparkling wine producer in California". Beautiful view of the valley.

MEADOWOOD RESORT

900 Meadowood Lane
St. Helena CA 94574
707.963.3646 • 800.458.8080
Fax: 707.963.3532

Croquet anyone? Meadowood, one of Napa Valley's most exquisite resorts, has the only professional croquet court in the Napa Valley and is the site of many tournaments. You can take lessons from the croquet pro, or enjoy any of the other activities at this luxurious 250-acre resort in a wooded park-like setting. Choose from tennis, golf, biking, swimming, hiking, sleeping or reading in the sun, or revitalizing yourself in the health spa.

In the quiet of the early morning, you may see deer wandering across the nine-hole golf course. Sumptuous breakfasts await early risers seven days a week. Meadowood's superb restaurants attract both locals and visitors from afar.

The resort's wine school offers unique wine and food courses. Not surprising considering Meadowood is home to the Napa Valley Vintners Association and each June hosts the prestigious Napa Valley Wine Auction — one of the most famous events of its kind in the world.

Meadowood is elegant, luxuriously comfortable, and convenient to many of the Napa Valley's most renown wineries. It's *the* place to stay upvalley.

AUBERGE DU SOLEIL

180 Rutherford Hill Rd.
Rutherford CA 94573
707.963.1211
800.348.5406
Fax: 707.963.8764

A renowned restaurant and 50 room inn. Even if you don't stay here, you can enjoy a $10 to $15 breakfast with a spectacular view as the morning fog gradually burns off revealing the vineyards on the valley below. Or order one of the excellent burgers and salads from their "deck menu" for lunch.

SILVERADO COUNTRY CLUB AND RESORT

1600 Atlas Peak Road
Napa CA 94558
707.257.0200 • 800.532.0500
Fax: 707.257.5400

1200 acres whose cornerstone is a mansion built in the 1870's. Two hundred and eighty deluxe cottage suites complete with living room, wood burning fireplace, full kitchen, master bedroom and bath, private patio or terrace. Nine swimming pools. Two championship 18-hole golf courses designed by Robert Trent Jones, Jr. Twenty-three tennis courts. Three outstanding restaurants. Live music in the bar. It's *the* place to stay in Napa. What else can we say?

STAG'S LEAP WINE CELLARS

5766 Silverado Trail
Napa CA 94558
707.944.2020
Hours: Daily 10:00am-4:00pm
Tasting: $3.00 (includes souvenir glass)

Stag's Leap staggered the international wine community — and particularly the French — when its 1973 Cabernet Sauvignon took first place in a blind wine tasting in Paris in 1976. The renowned (and very French) wine tasters were horrified that an upstart California winery would best France's finest wines. Some even tried to get their tasting notes back.

Stag's Leap Wine Cellars' place in history was secure. Other Napa Valley wineries have since won many awards in France and other international competitions, but Stag's Leap has never rested on its laurels, and continues to produce superb wines, including its celebrated Cask 23. It well deserves your visit.

SCENIC DRIVES

HIGHWAY 29

Every road in the Napa Valley is scenic. Some are just more scenic than others. Highway 29, the main road up the (westish) center of the valley, takes you through all the valley towns and right by some of the area's most famous wineries and restaurants. And from Napa to St. Helena it parallels the route of the Napa Valley Wine Train. Wave at the engineer and passengers. That's half the fun for everybody.

Passing through St. Helena, Highway 29 is called Main Street. Along most other stretches it's referred to as the Saint Helena Highway. In reality it's all Highway 29 — a divided highway from Napa to Yountville, and a two-lane highway (with frequent left-turn lanes) all the way from Yountville to Calistoga. Caltrans, the State of California's transportation department, would love to make "29" a divided highway the whole length of the valley, but the natives have fought valiantly and successfully to prevent this from happening. Even most of those who commute up or down the valley are willing to put up with the inconvenience of a two-lane road in order to preserve the beauty of the drive.

To get a full appreciation of the Napa Valley, you should definitely drive Highway 29, in one direction or the other.

THE SILVERADO TRAIL

The Silverado Trail runs along the east side of the valley. It goes outside most of the towns, and there are fewer wineries and much less traffic. Yet it still offers beautiful views, many wineries and quicker driving if you're in a hurry. Don't be in too much of a hurry, however. The view is too lovely and this road can be dangerous, because people drive much faster than on Highway 29 and seem to get more impatient, passing on stretches where it is unsafe to pass. Use caution and you'll enjoy "the Trail" immensely. We do.

The name "Silverado" comes from the road's history carrying quicksilver (mercury) wagons from the mines in northern Napa County. The quicksilver was eventually transported to the gold fields of California where it was used to separate gold from the ore or sand in which it was found. The Trail also led to the Silverado silver mine on Mt. St. Helena where years later Robert Louis Stevenson gathered the notes for his story *The Silverado Squatters*.

THE CROSS ROADS

Crossing the valley from east to west, and connecting Highway 29 with the Silverado Trail, are three major crossroads. Each road crosses the valley at the town which it's named after. They are: Yountville Cross Road, Oakville Cross Road, and Rutherford Cross Road. (Several other roads make this connection, too, but they don't quite have the flair that the crossroads do). Each road passes wineries and beautiful homes, and all offer gorgeous views. Try any one of these to get off the beaten path.

CUTTINGS WHARF ROAD

Don't be too disappointed if after turning off Highway 121/12 south of Napa, you follow the "Napa River Resorts" signs to Cuttings Wharf and have trouble finding the "resorts". Perhaps once there were resorts in this area, although there appears to be no historical record that this was ever the case. Still, it's a pleasant drive, taking you through some of Napa County's section of the Carneros wine district, famous for its Chardonnays and Pinot Noirs.

SOLANO AVENUE & WASHINGTON STREET

Between Yountville and Napa is an 8-mile stretch of divided highway. The highway provides beautiful views, but for more leisurely sightseeing we offer two tips. Northbound from Napa, turn right (east) at the Washington Street turnoff, then turn immediately left to go north again. Follow the frontage road to Yountville, enjoy the view of the vineyards by the side of the road, and take pictures of the beautiful views toward the mountains to the east.

Coming back at the end of the day, skip the divided highway again. Instead go west off Highway 29 at the Veterans Home turnoff, cross the tracks and turn left on the frontage road (Solano Avenue) to go south toward Napa. This will give you beautiful views of homes, vineyards and wineries to the west toward the Mayacamas Mountains. If this is at sunset, it's even more beautiful. Follow Solano into Napa and then, when you reach the business/ residential areas, turn back onto the highway again and continue your journey on the main highway.

YOUNT MILL ROAD

A beautiful drive that will take you from Yount Street in Yountville to Highway 29 north of town. You'll pass the site of the original mill built by town founder George Yount in 1836.

PLAN AHEAD

Some of Napa Valley's finest experiences require advance reservation. If you're able to plan ahead, it will enhance your Napa Valley visit.

CORPORATE EVENT & PERSONAL TOUR PLANNING

If you're bringing a corporate group to the valley, here are some companies that will assist you in making your visit both productive and enjoyable.

Alliance
1457 Calistoga Avenue
Napa CA 94559
707.257.1737 • Fax: 707.257.2001
Email: 73404.504@compuserve.com
Alliance can plan or assist with wine country tours, meetings, and events. Services also include programs for spouses, corporate gifts, and transportation.

Tim Mertz
800-409-1927
Event planning for business or private groups. The insider's insider, Tim specializes in private VIP tours at select wineries. He can also arrange group events at restaurants and wineries, and luncheons or candlelight dinners for groups at small exclusive winery estates, including special cave dining.

Wine & Dine Tours
P.O. Box 513
1109 Galleron Road
St. Helena CA 94574
707.963.8930 • 800.WINETOUR
Designs, organizes, and conducts winery tours and events for groups as small as two and as large as twenty-five thousand. Focusing on such things as wine and food pairing meals, off-the-beaten-path wineries, educational seminars, enology lectures, meet the winemaker special events, and cooking demonstrations.

FRENCH LAUNDRY RESTAURANT

6640 Washington
Yountville CA 94599
707.944.2380

Some people consider this the finest restaurant in the United States. Reservations should generally be made at least six months in advance.

GOOSECROSS CELLARS

1119 State Lane
Yountville CA 94599
707.944.1986 • 800.276.9210

Goosecross Cellars offers a free Wine Basics Class every Saturday morning
at 11:00 am. You'll learn all the wine jargon you need to make your way
through the Napa Valley, plus what to look for in wine, how to store and age
it, and all that fancy wine etiquette stuff (should I swirl, dump, gurgle or
spit?). A fun and informative class that includes a free class guidebook.
Registration required.

HAGAFEN CELLARS

Napa
707.252.0781

Established in 1979, Hagafen (meaning "the vine") Cellars is the only kosher
winery in the Napa Valley. Winemaker Ernie Weir turns out award-winning
wines, which have frequently been served at state occasions in the White
House. Tours are by appointment only. L'chaim.

MERRYVALE VINEYARDS

1000 Main St. (Highway 29)
St. Helena CA 94574
707.963.7777 • 800.326.6069
Hours: 10 am to 5:30 pm
Directions: Winery is south of the bridge leading into the heart of downtown
St. Helena and within walking distance from town.

Merryvale offers Saturday Morning Seminars. Each seminar focuses on wine
and its essential components - sugar, alcohol, acid and tannin. Merryvale
wines are tasted in conjunction with these basic ingredients to demonstrate
how they blend together to create balance in wines. But, more importantly,
you'll have a chance to map your own palate and find out about your likes
and dislikes. You'll find this an entertaining and educational experience.

Seminars are held from 10:30 am until noon every Saturday. The fee is
$10.00 per person. Reservations are required.

RUTHERFORD HILL WINERY

200 Rutherford Hill Road
Rutherford CA 94573
707.963.7194

An extensive system of wine caves, perhaps the largest in North America, is home to over 8,000 French oak barrels used in the age of Rutherford Hill's wine. It's also the site for Blending in the Caves, which allows participants to create their own blend of Rutherford Hill Merlot.

After a tour, your wine instructor will assist you by informing you about vineyard locations, varietal characteristics, flavor, taste, and a few basic principles of blending. Then, sampling three varietal wines taken directly from the barrel, you'll create your own blend that you will bottle and take home to enjoy. For a special experience, your group can enter team blends into a "Merlot Blend-Off" competition. Reservations required.

WINERY TOURS BY APPOINTMENT

Most small, out-of-the-way, family-owned wineries give tours only by appointment. These are the wineries that can be the most interesting, and that will give you a chance to actually talk with the winemaker himself.

To visit these wineries, call in advance. While you may be able to set up an appointment the same day, or the next day if you're spending the night in the valley, you're better off phoning before you even come to the valley.

Next time you're planning a trip, decide which small wineries make wines you particularly like, and phone them to see if you can set up a personalized tour and tasting at their facilities. It will be memorable. (By the way, this also works even for the larger wineries that give public tours. You might have your local wine shop call the winery and tell them you're a special customer who would like a private tour.)

NAPA WINE & LABEL

Las Cerezas Vineyards
800.409.1927

Impress your friends, create your own private wine label!

Napa Wine & Label of Las Cerezas Vineyards can create custom wine labels exclusively for you or your business. They've created labels for golf tournaments, weddings, anniversaries. . . even baby announcements. Their on-site graphic department can transform your ideas or original artwork into a custom label for your very own private wine offering, provided by them.

Located in St. Helena. Not open to the public, but private tastings can be arranged. Tell them Nutshell sent you.

LODGING RESERVATIONS

NAPA VALLEY TOURIST BUREAU

6488 Washington Street
Yountville CA 94599
707.944.1558

This is on the main street of Yountville, so you can stop by and visit in person. See them also about hot air ballooning, conferences, car rentals, and weddings.

WINE COUNTRY BED & BREAKFAST RESERVATIONS

PO Box 5059
Napa CA 94581
707.257.7757

NAPA VALLEY RESERVATIONS UNLIMITED

1819 Tanen Street
Napa CA 94559
707.252.1985 • 800.251.6272
Fax: 707.252.4585

BED & BREAKFAST INNS OF THE NAPA VALLEY

PO Box 2937
Yountville CA 94599
707.944.4444

HOTEL HOTLINE

707.963.8466• 800.499.8466 (California only)

B&B STYLE

707.942.2888 • 800.995.8884

The Napa Valley is filled with bed and breakfast inns, hotels, resorts and spas. The simplest way for you to find a place to spend the night is through one of the reservation services. They'll know which places have rooms available, and can recommend accommodations suitable for your needs. Plus there's no extra charge for their services.

A complete list of Napa Valley wineries is provided on **PAGE 79** of this book to assist in your planning.

ANNUAL, SEASONAL & OCCASIONAL EVENTS

These listings were not considered for the "100 Best" section because they're not regularly available, but they're well worth attending if you're here at the right time. Up-to-the-minute listings are available on-line at http://www.westsong.com— then click on "Calendar".

APRIL IN CARNEROS

800.825.9457
Annual open house and festival sponsored by wineries in the Carneros District.

CAROLS IN THE CAVES

707.224.4222
Weekends during November and December in the wine caves of various wineries.

David Auerbach, who should be declared a Napa Valley treasure, plays sacred music on rare and unusual instruments. As David says, "If you've heard of it, I probably don't play it." A rare treat.

CHAMBER MUSIC IN THE NAPA VALLEY

707.252.7122
Outstanding performances usually held in the beautiful and acoustically excellent First Methodist Church in Napa. Call for schedule.

CLOS PEGASE WINE/ART LECTURE

Calistoga
707.942.4981

Clos Pegase winery founder Jan Shrem gives a free monthly talk on "4,000

CHRISTMAS TREE FARMS

Big Ranch Tree Farm
2056 Big Ranch Road,
Napa CA 94558
707.224.0611

Bruderer's Christmas Tree Farm
3663 Solano Avenue,
Napa CA 94558
707.226.3502

Mount George Christmas Tree Farm
1053 Mount George Ave.
Napa CA 94558
707.224.3729

Napa Valley Christmas Tree Farm
2130 Big Ranch Road,
Napa CA 94558
707.252.1000

Years of Wine in Art" at the winery just south of Calistoga. Call for date and time of next lecture.

CONCOURS D'ELEGANCE

Silverado Country Club, Napa
510.428.3355

A lavish display of classic automobiles. Held in early June.

DOMAINE CHANDON BASTILLE DAY CELEBRATION

Domaine Chandon, Yountville
707.944.2280

Held every July 14.

DOMAINE CHANDON CABERNET CONCERT SERIES

Domaine Chandon, Yountville
707.944.2280

Held in January and February. Excellent well-known cabaret performers.

THE DREAMWEAVERS THEATRE

101 South Coombs
Napa CA 94559
707.255.5483

Napa's only non-profit live theater. Four shows a year.

FESTIVAL OF LIGHTS

Yountville
707.944.0904
December

Beautiful Christmas displays, music, entertainment.

HARVEST (CRUSH)

August, September, October

The grape harvest takes place every year in the early fall. Depending on the weather, it can start in early August for champagne grapes, which are picked at lower sugar levels. It picks up steam in late August and is in full swing during most of September and October. This is the time to actually see how wine is made. The stemmer-crushers are operating throughout the day, the fermentation tanks are full and bubbling with carbon dioxide, and gondolas overflowing with grapes are traveling along every countryside road in the valley.

HUMAN RACE

Silverado Country Club, Napa
707.252.6222
10K Run, 5K Walk

Every year in May. This is a popular run/walk for people from throughout the San Francisco Bay Area. It's a fundraiser for non-profit organizations throughout the Napa Valley and is organized by the Volunteer Center of Napa County.

JARVIS CONSERVATORY

1711 Main Street
Napa CA 94559
707.255.5445

An absolutely exquisite theater devoted to an art form little known in this country: Spanish opera, called "Zarzuela," something like a Spanish version of Gilbert & Sullivan. Situated in the building that once housed the Joseph Mathews distillery (and later winery), the Conservatory offers classes and public performances of zarzuela and other operatic music. If it were available every night, we'd list it in our 100 Best. But since the focus is on classes, and the performances are not held regularly, we've listed it in this section. If there's a performance happening while you're in the valley, give it a try.

FARMERS MARKETS

Chef's Market (Napa)
Napa Town Center
Downtown Napa
707.255.8073
Fridays, May - Oct.
2pm - 6pm, music and food till 9pm.

Fresh produce, beer, wine, food, specialty foods, fine art, kids' art, live entertainment, wine and food tastings, outdoor dining.

Farmers Market (Napa)
Downtown Napa in the parking lot on Pearl and West Streets, off Soscol.
707.252.7142
Tuesdays, May - Oct.
7:30am to noon

Fresh produce, baked goods, artisans. A popular event for locals and visitors who appreciate quality food.

Farmers Market (St. Helena)
Crane Park, St. Helena
707.252.2105
Fridays, May - Oct.
7:30 am - 11:30 am

At St. Helena High School turn west on Grayson, left on Crane. Specialty foods, master gardeners, local artisans.

LAND TRUST HIKES
Napa County Land Trust
1040 Main Street
Napa CA 94559
707.252.3270
Throughout the year

Hikes held throughout Napa County, usually at locations which are normally closed to the public.

MAGICAL MOONSHINE PUPPET THEATER
PO Box 2296
Yountville CA 94599
707.257.8007

This is another Napa Valley treasure that we would list in our 100 Best section if it were available more regularly. Unfortunately, performances are only held sporadically. Fortunately for locals, they're frequent enough to be a favorite, and held at locations throughout the valley. A wonderful experience for kids, no matter what their age.

MOUNTAIN MEN (SKYLINE PARK)
Skyline Park, Napa
707.252.0481

Mountain men in furs and deerskin with muzzle-loading rifles. An annual event, open to the public. Call the park to find out when this takes place.

NAPA VALLEY COLLEGE THEATRE
2277 Napa-Vallejo Highway
Napa CA 94558
707.253.3200
Web site: http://nvc.cc.ca.us/nvc/fp_arts.html
Just south of Napa at Imola and Soscol

The Napa Valley College Division of Fine and Performing Arts sponsors approximately 100 events each year: plays, musicals and concerts (choral, jazz, and instrumental), including events for young audiences.

Tickets at the NVC Cashier, Blumer's Music Center in Napa, and Main Street Books in St. Helena, or use Visa/MasterCard and phone the college for tickets. Free parking; wheelchair access.

NAPA COUNTY FAIR
1435 Oak Street
Calistoga CA 94515
707.942.5111

Always held over the 4th of July holiday

NAPA TOWN & COUNTRY FAIR
Napa Valley Exposition
Napa
707.253.4900

The really big fair in Napa County. Held in early August.

NAPA VALLEY ACADEMY AWARDS BENEFIT
Napa Valley Exposition
575 Third Street, Napa
707.257.8686

Held every year the night of the Academy Awards. Includes more than two dozen wine and food pairings from Napa Valley's finest wineries and restaurants. Dancing, silent auction, and big-screen simulcast of the Academy Awards. A very popular event that benefits local AIDS projects.

NAPA VALLEY MODEL RAILROAD CLUB
Napa Valley Exposition
Third Street Gate
Napa CA 94559
707.253.8428
Open Friday evenings from 7:30 on and during major fairground events.

This elaborate model railroad occupies a 3600 square foot room at the Napa Fairgrounds.

The "Napa Valley Northern" runs from Napa north through Lake County with northbound connections to Portland, and southbound connections to Stockton. The layout has more than 1500 feet of track and the time period is from 1940 to present. Great for kids and railroad fans of any age.

Napa Valley Music Festival

PO Box 10227
Napa CA 94581
707.252.4813

Held for three days in September at Skyline Park in Napa.

It's the largest annual musical event held in Napa County, and includes over 20 contemporary acts, three days of workshops, three main stages, the Emerging Songwriter Showcase, a Saturday morning kids' concert, continuous open mikes, and plenty of opportunities for aspiring singer/songwriters to meet with some of the most famous songwriters of the North American musical scene. Folk, gospel, country, Cajun, Native American, Celtic, South American, bluegrass, blues, Chicano, jug band and more can be heard as the festivities continue virtually around the clock. Camping, jamming, abundant food, beverages, wine tasting, and crafts round out this exceptional celebration of song.

Napa Valley Mustard Festival

707.942.9762

Held in February and March at locations throughout the valley.

Napa Valley Shakespeare Festival

Held in July at Charles Krug Winery, St. Helena
707.253.3208

A semi-professional troupe of actors perform outdoors in the parklike setting on a permanent stage. Seating is on the oak-shaded two-acre lawn next to the Carriage House built in 1881. Picnics are a tradition, but all beverages must be purchased on the premises. All performances start at 7 pm. Tickets are available at the gate. A 10% discount for dinner at Pairs or Spring Street Restaurants in St. Helena is available by presenting the evening's tickets. Box suppers are available by advance order. 5 day advance reservations and choice of three menus. Low-back lawn chair rental is $3. Free parking and wheelchair access.

Napa Valley Symphony

2407 California Boulevard
Napa CA 94558
707.226.6872

Maestro Asher Raboy and his predecessors have put together an outstanding group of musicians. Most concerts are held in Lincoln Theater at the Veterans Home in Yountville. There's also an annual free concert by the river at Veterans Park in downtown Napa. Call the Symphony for a schedule of all performances.

NAPA VALLEY WINE AUCTION

1091 Larkmead Lane
Calistoga CA 94515
707.963.5246

A world-famous wine event held each year in early June at the Meadowood Resort in St. Helena. Very elegant, very expensive. Admission by prior registration only.

NAPA VALLEY WINE FESTIVAL

Napa Valley Exposition
November

This is a major annual event sponsored by the Napa Valley Unified Education Foundation as a benefit for Napa public schools. Over 50 wineries participate, so it's a unique opportunity to try a wide variety of Napa Valley wines.

OGIM (OH GOSH!! IT'S MONDAY)

Domaine Chandon
Yountville
707.944.2280
June and July

Concerts with a wide, wide range: jazz, country, rock, world beat and more. Held on the upper terrace of Domaine Chandon's visitors' center. Gates open at 6:30 pm for first-come seating. Chandon sparkling wines and non-alcoholic beverages available for purchase during each performance. No one under 21 admitted.

Tickets available starting in May. Benefits the Napa Valley Opera House and the Arts Council of Napa Valley.

ROBERT MONDAVI SUMMER FESTIVAL

Robert Mondavi Winery
Oakville CA
707.226.1395
June, July and August

Margrit Biever Mondavi, vice president of cultural affairs at the Robert Mondavi Winery and wife of the founder, has made this her pet project since 1969. Concerts are open-air, held on the winery's main lawn. Most concerts begin at 7 pm, with gates open at 5 pm for picnicking.

1996's entertainment lineup gives an idea of the outstanding quality of the performers: Harry Belafonte, New Orleans' Preservation Hall Jazz Band, Etta James, Al Jarreau and Lou Rawls.

Wine and cheese tastings are offered at intermission. Proceeds go to the Napa Valley Symphony League. Tickets range from $30–$45 (same for adults and children), depending on the performer. While children are allowed, we've seldom seen any there.

It's an elegantly casual affair, with most attending in jeans and shorts but some finely dressed. Picnic baskets brought by guests range from French bread and cheese to elegantly prepared meals served with fine china and crystal. It's great fun and outstanding entertainment. Tickets, which go on sale the end of April, go fast. They're available at the winery and all BASS outlets. A sign at the front of the winery easily visible from Highway 29 shows the season's schedule and ticket availability.

SOCIETY FOR CREATIVE ANACHRONISM
Skyline Park, Napa
707.252.0481

The Society for Creative Anachronism (SCA) meets annually at Skyline Park in Napa for a day of jousting, swordsmanship, wenching, dining and general rollicking fun. Open to the public for a small donation. Call Skyline Park to find the date of the SCA's next visit.

VALLEY MEN WHO COOK
Upvalley location
707.255.5911

Held on Father's Day each year. Amateur but well known chefs from around the valley compete in a wide variety of food categories. A very popular and fun event.

VETERANS HOME FOURTH OF JULY FIREWORKS
Veterans Home, Yountville

At dusk every Fourth of July. The biggest fireworks display in the valley.

VICTORIAN HOLIDAY CANDLELIGHT TOUR
December
707.255.1836
Annual tour of some of Napa's most beautifully restored Victorian homes. Sponsored by Napa County Landmarks.

WHITE BARN

St. Helena
707.963.7002

Local theatrical and musical performances held
throughout the year.

WINE AND CRAFTS FAIR

Downtown Napa
707.257.0322
September
Wine tasting, crafts, food, entertaining. The big
street fair of the year.

WINE COUNTRY FILM FESTIVAL

Every July/August in both Napa and Sonoma
Valleys.
707.935.3456 for program information, advance
tickets to al fresco screenings, and passes. Tickets
are available at BASS outlets.

Founded in 1986, the Wine Country Film Festival
stretches over four weekends in July and August.
It has a true, casual, wine country feeling. Many of
the films are screened outdoors, at Rutherford Hill
Winery in the Napa Valley and Viansa Winery in
the Sonoma Valley. Other films are screened
indoors at the Cameo Cinema in St. Helena and
the Uptown Theater in Napa. Tickets can be
purchased at showtime and range from $6–$20. A
Weekend Pass gives reserved seating for all films
and events on a given weekend. Silver Passes,
which are $100, ensure reserved seating for every
film in the month-long festival.

The program always includes new features from
major studios and the latest in independently
produced features, documentaries and shorts from
around the world. It has premiered such films as
"A Fish Called Wanda", "Honeymoon in Vegas",
"sex, lies and videotape", and "Married to the
Mob", and held tributes to such stars as Anthony
Quinn and Gregory Peck.

Just Outside the Napa Valley

They're not in the Napa Valley but they're close by and might interest you. Each of these destinations is about a 20 minute drive from downtown Napa.

Marine World /Africa USA

Marine World Parkway
Vallejo CA 94589
707.643.6722
Open all year, Wednesday through Sunday from 9:30 am to 5 pm, and every day during the summer from 9:30 am to 6:30 pm (Memorial Day to Labor Day).

Whales, tigers, elephants, sharks, kangaroos, water-skiing shows, trained seals, giraffes, butterflies and scads of other animals and performances. It's probably the premier place in the entire San Francisco Bay Area for a family outing.

Anheuser-Busch Brewery

3101 Bush Drive
Fairfield CA 94533
707.429.7595
Open year-round Tuesday through Saturday from 9 am to 4 pm. Tours depart on the hour.

The world's largest brewer. Enjoy samples of fine beers and snacks. Visit the production floor to see packaging lines that fill thousands of cans and bottles every minute.

JELLY BELLY

Herman Goelitz Candy Company
2400 North Watney Way
Fairfield CA
800.522.3267

Take Interstate 80 north toward Sacramento. At
Fairfield, exit freeway at Highway 12/Chadbourne
Road, and exit at Chadbourne. Turn right at stop
sign onto Chadbourne, then left onto Courage
Drive. Turn left onto North Watney Way.
Tours Monday through Friday from 9 am to 2 pm.
Closed holidays, April 1, and the last week of June
through the first week of July.

Ronald Reagan's favorite snack. The first jelly
beans in outer space. And the makers of another
long-time favorite, Candy Corn. The factory makes
up to 40,000,000 jelly beans a day and sells
enough each year to circle the earth's equator 2 1/2
times. It's the only place in the world where you
can buy Belly Flops®, beans that don't meet
Goelitz's high standards for size or color, but
they're still delicious. A fun tour and great for kids.

VALLEJO FERRY

Downtown Vallejo
707.643.3779

The ferry's route takes
you the length of San
Pablo Bay, beneath the
Richmond/San Rafael
Bridge, along the scenic
shoreline of Marin
County, past historic
Angel Island (most
ferries stop here and it's
a great place for hiking
and picnicking) and on
to the Ferry Building or
Pier 39 in San Fran-
cisco. It's a beautiful
trip offering views of
San Francisco Bay and
its shoreline that you'll
never see any other way.
A great trip for adults
and kids.

Offering refreshments,
a full-service bar, and
all-inclusive packages
for Marine World/
Africa USA and the
Napa Valley Wine
Train.

Kids' Favorites

Sights and activities of special interest to children. (Watching parents taste wine can get boring pretty quickly.) See the "100 Best" section for specific information on each of these listings.

- Bothe-Napa Valley State Park (Calistoga)
- Napa Firefighters Museum (Napa)
- Napa Valley Museum (St. Helena)
- Napa Valley Wine Train (Napa)
- Old Bale Mill (St. Helena)
- Old Faithful Geyser (Calistoga)
- Napa Valley Riverboat Company (Napa)
- Rutherford Grill (Rutherford)
- Seguin Moreau Cooperage (Napa)
- Sterling Vineyards (and airtram) (Calistoga)
- Swimming Pools at Spas (Calistoga)
- The Spot (St. Helena)
- Yountville Park (Yountville)

Outside Napa Valley
- Jelly Belly (Fairfield)
- Marine World/Africa USA (Vallejo)

NAPA VALLEY WINERIES

We've included this list so you can track down a favorite winery. Not all of these wineries have tours or onsite sales. Most that do have them by appointment only. To avoid disappointment, call first to find out hours and availability of tours.

Acacia Winery
2750 Las Amigas Rd., Napa
707.226.9991

Aetna Springs Cellars
7227 Pope Valley Rd.,
Pope Valley
707.965.2675

Alatera Vineyards
2170 Hoffman Ln., Yountville
707.944.2620

Aloise Francisco Vineyards
1054 Bayview Ave., Napa
707.252.4005

Altamura Winery
4240 Silverado Tr., Napa
707.253.2000

Amizetta Vineyards Winery
1099 Greenfield Rd,St. Helena
707.963.1460

S. Anderson Vineyard
1473 Yountville Crossroad,
Yountville
707.944.8642

Anderson's Conn Valley
Vineyards
680 Rossi Rd., St Helena
707.963.8600

Araujo Estate Wines
2155 Picket Rd, Calistoga
707.942.6061

Arroyo Winery
2361 Greenwood Ave., Calistoga
707.942.6995

Atlas Peak Vineyards
3700 Soda Canyon Rd., Napa
707.252.7971

Azalea Springs
4301 Azalea Springs Way,
Calistoga
707.942.4811

Barnett Vineyards
4070 Spring Mountain. Rd.,
St. Helena
707.963.0109

Bayview Cellars
1202 Main St., Napa
707.255.8544

Beaucanon
1695 S. St. Helena Hwy.,
St. Helena
707.967.3520

Beaulieu Vineyard
1960 St. Helena Hwy., Rutherford
707.967.5411

Benessere Vineyards
1010 Big Tree Rd., St. Helena
707.963.5853

Beringer Vineyards
2000 Main St., St. Helena
707.963.4812

Bernard Pradel Cellars
2100 Hoffmann Ln., Yountville
707.944.8720

Bouchaine Vineyards
1075 Buchli Station Rd., Napa
707.252.9065

Buehler Vineyards
820 Greenfield Rd., St. Helena
707.963.2155

Burgess Cellars
1108 Deer Park Rd., St. Helena
707.963.4766

Cain Vineyards & Winery
3800 Langtry Rd., St. Helena
707.963.1616

Cakebread Cellars
8300 St Helena Hwy., Rutherford
707.963.5221

Calafia Cellars
629 Fulton Ln., St. Helena
707.963.5221

Carneros Alambic Distillery
1250 Cuttings Wharf Rd, Napa
707.253.9055

Carneros Creek Winery
1285 Dealy Ln., Napa
707.253.9463

Casa Nuestra Winery
3451 Silverado Tr. N., St. Helena
707.963.5783

Caymus Vineyards
8700 Conn Creek Rd., St Helena
707.967.3010

Chappellet Vineyard
1581 Sage Canyon Rd., St. Helena
707.963.7136

Charles Krug Winery
2800 St. Helena Hwy. N,
St Helena
707.963.2761

Chateau Boswell
3468 Silverado Tr., St. Helena
707.963.5472

Chateau Chevre Winery
2030 Hoffmann Ln., Yountville
707.944.2184

Chateau Montelena Winery
1429 Tubbs Ln., Calistoga
707.942.5105

Chateau Potelle
3875 Mount Veeder Rd., Napa
707.255.9440

Chateau Woltner
3500 Silverado Tr., St. Helena
707.963.1744

Chiles Valley Vineyard
2676 Lower Chiles Valley Rd.,
St. Helena
707.963.7294

Chimney Rock Winery
5350 Silverado Tr., Napa
707.257.2641

Clos Du Val Wine Co., Ltd.
5330 Silverado Tr., Napa
707.259.2220

Clos Pegase Winery
1060 Dunaweal Ln., Calistoga
707.942.4981

Codorniu Napa
1345 Henry Rd., Napa
707.224.1668

Colgin-Schrader Cellars
7830-40 St. Helena Hwy.
Oakville
707.524.4445

Conn Creek Winery
8711 Silverado Tr., St. Helena
707.963.5133

Cosentino Winery
7415 St. Helena Hwy, Yountville
707.944.1220

Costello Vineyards Winery
1200 Orchard Ave., Napa
707.252.8483

Cuvaison Winery
4550 Silverado Tr., Calistoga
707.942.6266

Dalla Valle Vineyards
7776 Silverado Tr., Yountville
707.944.2676

David Arthur Vineyards
1521 Sage Canyon Rd, St. Helena
707.963.5190

Deer Park Winery
1000 Deer Park Rd., Deer Park
707.963.5411

DeMoor Winery
7481 St. Helena Hwy., Yountville
707.944.2565

Diamond Creek Vineyards
1500 Diamond Mountain Rd.,
Calistoga
707.942.6926

Diamond Mountain Vineyard
2121 Diamond Mountain Rd.,
Calistoga
707.942.0707

Domain Hill & Mayes
1775 Lincoln Avenue, Napa
707.224.6565

Domaine Carneros by Taittinger
1240 Duhig Rd., Napa
707.257.0101

Domaine Chandon
California Dr., Yountville
707.944.2280

Domaine Charbay Winery &
Distillery
4001 Spring Mountain Rd., St.
Helena
707.963.9327

Domaine Montreax
4101 Big Ranch Rd., Napa
707.252.9380

Domaine Napa Winery
1155 Mee Ln., St. Helena
707.963.1666

Dominus Estate
2570 Napanook Rd., Yountville
707.944.8954

Duckhorn Vineyards
3027 Silverado Tr. N,St. Helena
707.963.7108

Dunn Vineyards
805 White Cottage Rd., Angwin
707.965.3642

Dutch Henry Winery
4300 Silverado Tr., Calistoga
707.942.5771

Edgewood Estates
401 St. Helena Hwy. St. Helena
707.963.2335

Ehlers Grove Winery
3222 Ehlers Ln., St. Helena
707.963.3200

Eisele V & L Family Estate
3080 Lower Chiles Valley Rd.,
St. Helena
707.965.2260

El Molino Winery
P.O. Box 306, St. Helena
707.963.3632

Elkhorn Peak Cellars
200 Polson Rd., Napa
707.255.0504

Elyse Wine Cellars
PO Box 83, Rutherford
707.963.5496

Etude Wines
4101 Big Ranch Rd., Napa
707.257.5300

Far Niente Winery
P.O. Box 327, Oakville
707.944.2861

Farella-Park Vineyards
PO Box 5217, Napa
707.254.9489

Flora Springs Wine Co.
1978 W. Zinfandel Ln., St. Helena
707.963.5711

Folie a Deux
3070 N. St. Helena Hwy.,
St. Helena
707.963.1160

Forest Hill Vineyard
P.O. Box 96, St. Helena
707.963.7229

Franciscan Oakville Estate
1178 Galleron Rd., Rutherford
707.963.7111

Franciscan Vineyards
1178 Galleron Rd., Rutherford
707.963.7111

Freemark Abbey Winery
3022 N. St. Helena Hwy.,
St. Helena
707.963.9694

Frisinger Cellars
2277 Dry Creek Rd., Napa
707.255.3749

Frog's Leap Winery
8815 Conn Creek Rd.,
Rutherford
707.963.4704

Girard Winery
7717 Silverado Tr., Oakville
707.944.8577

Goosecross Cellars
1119 State Ln., Yountville
707.944.1986

Grace Family Vineyards
1210 Rockland Dr., St. Helena
707.963.0808

Graeser Winery
255 Petrified Forest Rd.,
Calistoga
707.942.4437

Green & Red Vineyard
3208 Chiles Pope Valley Rd.,
St. Helena
707.965.2346

Grgich Hills Cellars
1829 St. Helena Hwy.,
Rutherford
707.963.2784

Groth Vineyards & Winery
750 Oakville Cross Rd.,
Oakville
707.944.0290

Hagafen Cellars
PO Box 3035, Napa
707.252.0781

Hakusan Sake Gardens
1 Executive Way, Napa
707.258.6160

Hanson-Hsieh Vineyard
1019 Dry Creek Rd., Napa
707.257.2632

Harlan Estate Winery
PO Box 352, Oakville
707.944.1441

Harrison Vineyards
1527 Sage Canyon Rd., St.
Helena
707.963.8271

Hartwell Vineyards
5795 Silverado Tr., Napa
707.255.4269

Havens Wine Cellars
2055 Hoffman Ln., Yountville
707.945.0921

Heitz Wine Cellars
500 Taplin Rd., St Helena
707.963.3542

The Hess Collection
4411 Redwood Rd., Napa
707.255.1144

Honig Cellars
850 Rutherford Rd., Rutherford
707.963.5618

Jaeger Inglewood Cellar
PO Box 388, Rutherford
707.963.1875

Jarvis Vineyards
2970 Monticello Rd., Napa
707.255.5280

Joseph Phelps Vineyards
200 Taplin Rd., St. Helena
707.963.2745

Joya Wine Company
880 Vallejo St., Napa
707.254.9548

Karl Lawrence Cellars
4541 Monticello Rd., Napa
707.255.2843

Kate's Vineyard
5211 Big Ranch Rd., Napa
707.255.2644

Kornell Cellars
PO Box 1012, St. Helena
707.942.0859

La Vieille Montagne
3851 Spring Mountain Rd., St.
Helena
707.963.9059

Lakespring Winery
2055 Hoffman Ln., Yountville
707.944.2475

Lamborn Family Vineyards
2075 Summit Lake Drive,
Angwin
707.965.2811

Larkmead Kornell Champagne
Cellars
1091 Larkmead Ln., St. Helena
707.942.0859

Larkmead Vineyards
1145 Larkmead Ln., Calistoga
707.942.6605

Livingston Wines
1895 Cabernet Ln., St. Helena
707.963.2120

Los Hermanos Vineyards
1000 Pratt Ave., St. Helena
707.963.7115

Louis Corthay Winery
996 Galleron Rd., St. Helena
707.963.2384

Louis M. Martini Winery
St. Helena Hwy., St. Helena
707.963.2736

Mario Perelli-Minetti Winery
1443 Silverado Tr.,
St. Helena
707.963.8762

Markham Vineyards
2812 N. St. Helena Hwy.,
St. Helena
707.963.5292

Mayacamus Vineyards
1155 Lokoya Rd., Napa
707.224.4030

Merryvale Vineyards
1000 Main, St. Helena
707.963.7777

Milat Vineyards
1091 St. Helena Hwy.,
St. Helena
707.963.0758

Mont St. John Cellars
5400 Old Sonoma Rd., Napa
707.255.8864

Monticello Vineyards
4242 Big Ranch Rd., Napa
707.253.2802

Montreaux
4242 Big Ranch Rd., Napa
707.252.9380

Moon Vineyards
3315 Sonoma Highway, Napa
707.226.2642

Moss Creek Winery
6015 Steele Canyon Rd., Napa
707.252.1295

Mt. Veeder Winery & Vineyards
1999 Mt. Veeder Rd., Napa
707.224.4039

Mumm Napa Valley
8445 Silverado Tr., Napa
800.95V.INTAGE

Napa Valley Port Cellars
736 California Blvd., Napa
707.257.7777

Napa Valley Vintners
Association
PO Box 141, St. Helena
707.963.0148

Napa Wine Company
1133 Oakville Cross Rd.,
Oakville
707.944.1710

Newlan Vineyards & Winery
5225 Solano Ave., Napa
707.257.2399

Newton Vineyard
2555 Madrona Av,
St. Helena
707.963.9000

Nichelini Winery
2950 Sage Canyon Rd.,
St. Helena
707.963.0717

Niebaum-Coppola Estate
Winery
PO Box 208, Rutherford
707.963.9435

Oakford Vineyards
PO Box 150, Oakville
707.945.0445

Oakville Ranch Vineyards
7781 Silverado Tr., Napa
415.284.1620

One Vineyard
St Helena
707.963.1123

Opus One Winery
7900 St Helena Highway,
Oakville
707.944.9442

Pahlmeyer
PO Box 2410, Napa
707.255.2321

Paradigm Winery
683 Dwyer Rd., Oakville
707.944.1683

Peju Province
8466 St. Helena Hwy.,
Rutherford
707.963.3600

Philip Togni Vineyard
3780 Spring Mountain Rd., St.
Helena
707.963.3731

Pine Ridge Winery
5901 Silverado Tr., Napa
707.252.9777

Plam Vineyards
6200 Washington St, Yountville
707.944.1102

Pope Valley Cellars
6613 Pope Valley Rd.,
Pope Valley
707.965.1438

Prager Winery & Port Works
1281 Lewelling Ln., St. Helena
707.963.7678

Pride Mountain Vineyards
Spring Mountain Rd.,
St. Helena
707.963.4949

Quail Ridge Cellars &
Vineyards
1960 St. Helena Highway,
Rutherford
707.257.1712

Quintessa
PO Box 407, Rutherford
707.963.7111

Raymond Vineyard & Cellar
849 Zinfandel Ln., St. Helena
707.963.3141

Ritchie Creek Vineyard
4024 Spring Mountain Rd.,
St. Helena
707.963.4661

Robert Keenan Winery
3660 Spring Mountain. Rd.,
St. Helena
707.963.9177

Robert Mondavi Winery
7801 St. Helena Hwy., Oakville
707.226.1335

Robert Pecota Winery
P.O. Box 303, Calistoga
707.942.6625

Robert Pepi Winery
7585 St. Helena Hwy, Yountville
707.944.2807

Robert Sinskey Vineyards
6320 Silverado Tr., Yountville
707.944.9090

Rombauer Vineyards
3522 Silverado Tr., St. Helena
707.967.5120

Round Hill Vineyards
1680 Silverado Tr.,
St. Helena
707.963.9503

Rustridge Winery
2910 Lower Chiles Valley Rd.,
St. Helena
707.965.2871

Rutherford Grove Winery
1673 St. Helena Highway,
Rutherford
707.963.0544

Rutherford Hill Winery
200 Rutherford Hill Rd.,
Rutherford
707.963.7194

Saintsbury
1500 Los Carneros Ave., Napa
707.252.0592

San Pietro Vara Vineyard &
Wine Company
1171 Tubbs Ln., Calistoga
707.942.0937

Schramsberg Vineyards
Schramsberg Rd., Calistoga
707.942.4558

Seavey Vineyards
1310 Conn Valley Rd,
St. Helena
707.963.8339

Sequoia Grove Vineyards
8338 S. St. Helena Hwy.,
Rutherford
707.944.2945

Shafer Vineyards
6154 Silverado Tr., Napa
707.944.2877

Signorello Vineyards
4500 Silverado Tr., Napa
707.255.5990

Silver Oak Cellars
915 Oakville Cross Rd.,
Oakville
707.944.8808

Silverado Hills Cellars
3103 Silverado Tr., Napa
707.253.9306

Silverado Vineyards
6121 Silverado Tr., Napa
707.257.1770

Smith-Madrone Vineyards
4022 Spring Mountain Rd.,
St. Helena
707.963.2283

Spottswoode Winery
1902 Madrona Ave.,
St. Helena
707.963.0134

Spring Mountain Vineyard
2805 Spring Mountain Rd,
St. Helena
707.967.4188

St. Andrews Winery
2921 Silverado Tr., Napa
707.259.2200

St. Clement Vineyards
2867 St. Helena Hwy.,
St. Helena
707.963.7221

St. Supéry Wine Discovery
Center & Winery
8440 St. Helena Hwy.,
Rutherford
707.963.4507

Stag's Leap Wine Cellars
5766 Silverado Tr., Napa
707.944.2020

Stag's Leap Winery
6150 Silverado Tr., Napa
707.944.1303

Staglin Family Vineyard
P.O. Box 680, Rutherford
707.963.1749

Star Hill Winery
1075 Shadybrook Ln., Napa
707.255.1957

Steltzner
5998 Silverado Tr., Napa
707.252.7272

Sterling Vineyards
1111 Dunaweal Ln., Calistoga
800.95VINTAGE

Stonegate Winery
1183 Dunaweal Ln., Calistoga
707.942.6500

Stony Hill Vineyard
3331 N. St. Helena Hwy., Napa
707.963.2636

Storybook Mountain Winery
3835 Hwy. 128, Calistoga
707.942.5310

Strack Vineyard
4120 St. Helena Hwy., Napa
707.224.5100

Stratford Winery
1472 Railroad Ave., St. Helena
707.963.3200
Streblow Vineyards
1455 Summit Lake Drive,
Angwin
707.963.5892

Sullivan Vineyards Winery
1090 Galleron Rd.,
Rutherford
707.963.9646

Summit Lake Vineyards &
Winery
2000 Summit Lake Drive,
Angwin
707.965.2488

Sutter Home Winery
277 St. Helena Hwy.,
St. Helena
707.963.3104

Swanson Vineyards
1271 Manley Ln., Rutherford
707.944.1642

Tongi Philip Vineyard
3780 Spring Mountain Rd.,
St. Helena
707.963.3731

Traulsen Vineyards
2250 Lake County Hwy.,
Calistoga
707.942.0283

Trefethen Vineyards
1160 Oak Knoll Ave., Napa
707.255.7700

Truchard Vineyards
3234 Old Sonoma Rd., Napa
707.253.7153

Tudal Winery
1015 Big Tree Rd., St. Helena
707.963.3947

Tulocay Winery
1426 Coombsville Rd., Napa
707.255.4064

Turley Wine Cellars
3358 St. Helena Hwy.,
St. Helena
707.963.0940

Turnbull Wine Cellars
8210 St. Helena Hwy., Oakville
707.963.5839

V. Sattui Winery
S. St. Helena Hwy., St. Helena
707.963.7774

Van Der Heyden Vineyards &
Winery
4057 Silverado Tr., Napa
707-257-0130

Venge Vineyards
7802 Money Rd., Oakville
707.944.1305

Viader Vineyards
1120 Deer Park Rd.,
Deer Park
707.963.3816

Vichon Winery
1595 Oakville Grade, Oakville
707.944.2811

Villa Encinal
620 Oakville Cross Rd, Oakville
707.944.1465

Villa Helena Winery
1455 Inglewood Av, St. Helena
707.963.4334

Villa Mt. Eden Winery
PO Box 350, St. Helena
707.944.2414

Vincent Arroyo Winery
2361 Greenwood Ave, Calistoga
707.942.6995

Vine Cliff Winery
7400 Silverado Tr., Yountville
707.944.1364

Volker Eisele Family Estate
3080 Lower Chiles Valley Rd.,
St. Helena
707.965.2260

Von Strasser Winery
1510 Diamond Mountain Rd.,
Calistoga
707.942.0930

Wermuth Winery
3942 Silverado Tr., Calistoga
707.942.5924

Whitehall Lane Winery
1563 S. St. Helena Hwy.,
St. Helena
707.963.9454

Whitford Cellars
4047 East 3rd Ave., Napa
707.257.7065

William Hill Winery
1761 Atlas Peak Rd., Napa
707.224.4477

Winter Creek Winery
PO Box 2847, Napa
707.252.8677

Woltner Estates Winery
150 White Cottage Rd. South,
Angwin
707.965.2445

Yverdon Vineyards
3787 Spring Mtn. Rd.,
St. Helena
707.963.4270

ZD Wines
8383 Silverado Tr., Napa
707.963.5188

INDEX

A

B

C

D

E

F

L

M

N

O

P

R

S

T

U

V

W

Y

Z

WESTSONG

THE COMPLETE GUIDE TO THE NAPA VALLEY

Web Site: www.westsong.com

Westsong is a free online directory to the Napa Valley that offers just about any information a visitor might need. (Except, of course, certain of the information contained in this handy, compact little book which is much easier for you to carry around than a computer).

Westsong is primarily a service for Napa Valley residents, yet it also provides the most complete Napa Valley visitor information of any site on the Internet. The reason is that Westsong lists *every* Napa Valley Web page, while other Web sites pretty much limit their listings to Web pages paid for by their own clients.

In that sense, Westsong - The Website is similar to this book. Neither has content influenced by advertising. The other similarity, of course, is that Westsong created both. Book and Website work together to provide you, the visitor, with all the information you need to plan and enjoy your visit to the Napa Valley.

NAPA VALLEY IN A NUTSHELL

An Insider's Guide to the 100 Best Napa Valley Experiences

Order Form

For Yourself - or a Friend

Ship To:

Company Name _____

Name _____

Address _____

City _____ **State/Prov** _____

Postal Code (ZIP) _____ **Country** _____

Telephone (optional) _____

Email (optional) _____

Please send me (or my friend):

_____ Copies of *Napa Valley in a Nutshell* @ $US 5.95 each $ _____

California residents add 7.75% tax $_____

Postage and handling
$3.00 first book, $2.00 each additional book $_____
(Non-continental U.S. residents please add appropriate additional amount for postage)

Total amount enclosed $_____

Payment by cheque or money order only. Make payable to:

Westsong
PO Box 2254
Napa CA 94558

If your order is a gift, write a message here:

_____

_____

Thanks for Your Order!

Visit us on the Web at www.westsong.com/pub

Napa Valley in a Nutshell

An Insider's Guide to the 100 Best Napa Valley Experiences

Order Form

For Yourself - or a Friend

Ship To:

Company Name _____

Name _____

Address _____

City _____ **State/Prov** _____

Postal Code (ZIP) _____ **Country** _____

Telephone (optional) _____

Email (optional) _____

Please send me (or my friend):

_____ Copies of *Napa Valley in a Nutshell* @ $US 5.95 each $ _____

California residents add 7.75% tax $_____

Postage and handling
$3.00 first book, $2.00 each additional book $_____
<small>(Non-continental U.S. residents please add appropriate additional amount for postage)</small>

Total amount enclosed $_____

Payment by cheque or money order only. Make payable to:

Westsong
PO Box 2254
Napa CA 94558

If your order is a gift, write a message here:

_____

_____

Thanks for Your Order!

Visit us on the Web at www.westsong.com/pub